BASIC
English
Grammar

FOURTH EDITION

VOLUME B with Essential Online Resources

Betty S. Azar
Stacy A. Hagen

Basic English Grammar, Fourth Edition
Volume B

Azar Associates: Shelley Hartle, Editor, and Sue Van Etten, Manager

Pearson Education, 221 River Street, Hoboken, NJ 07030

Staff credits: The people who made up the *Basic English Grammar, Fourth Edition, Volume B* team, representing editorial, production, design, and manufacturing, are, Dave Dickey, Nancy Flaggman, Amy McCormick, Robert Ruvo, and Marian Wassner.

Text composition: S4Carlisle Publishing Services

Illustrations: Don Martinetti—pages 266, 267, 278, 279, 281, 283, 286, 287, 288, 290, 292, 293, 305, 312, 320, 322, 323, 327, 329, 330, 331, 332, 340, 348, 361, 363, 365, 366, 368, 370, 376, 377, 378, 379, 380, 383, 386, 393, 398, 401, 402, 407, 411, 416, 417, 418, 419, 420, 421, 428, 431, 432, 434, 441, 447, 453, 454, 455, 456, 457, 458, 470, 471, 475, 479, 488

Chris Pavely—pages 270, 272, 274, 275, 280, 290, 291, 292, 295, 300, 304, 307, 310, 313, 315, 325, 334, 335, 336, 337, 343, 345, 352, 353, 354, 359, 362, 363, 375, 377, 391, 396, 397, 399, 400, 413, 427, 430, 431, 440, 445, 449, 466, 469

Photo Credits: Page 296 dieKleinert/Alamy; p. 297 Aaron Alex/Alamy; p. 367 Alexander Kaludov/Fotolia; p. 382 Christos Georghiou/Fotolia.

Printed in the United States of America

ISBN 10: 0-13-466017-X
ISBN 13: 978-0-13-466017-2

2 2020

To Shelley Hartle

For her watchful eye, her vast expertise,
her indefatigable good cheer

Contents

Preface to the Fourth Edition

Basic English Grammar is a developmental skills text for beginning English language learners. It uses a grammar-based approach integrated with communicative methodologies to promote the development of all language skills in a variety of ways. Starting from a foundation of understanding form and meaning, students engage in meaningful communication about real actions, real things, and their own lives in the classroom context. Grammar tasks are designed to encourage both fluency and accuracy.

The eclectic approach and abundant variety of exercise material remain the same as in the earlier editions, but this fourth edition incorporates new ways and means. In particular:

- **CORPUS-INFORMED CONTENT**
  Based on corpus research, grammar content has been added, deleted, or modified to reflect discourse patterns. New information highlighting differences between spoken and written English has been added to the charts, and students practice more frequently used structures. We have been careful to keep the information manageable for beginning students.

- **PRESENTATION OF KEY GRAMMAR**
  Chapter 15 (in earlier editions of *BEG*) has been moved to Chapter 6 of this edition in order to teach possessive forms earlier and present all pronouns together.

- **WARM-UP EXERCISES FOR THE GRAMMAR CHARTS**
  Newly created for the fourth edition, these innovative exercises precede the grammar charts and introduce the point(s) to be taught. They have been carefully crafted to help students *discover* the target grammar as they progress through each warm-up exercise. The warm-up exercises can help the teacher assess how much explanation and practice students will need.

- **MICRO-PRACTICE**
  At the beginning level, a single grammar structure (e.g. basic pronouns and possessives) sometimes needs to be presented in several steps. Additional exercises have been created to give students more incremental practice.

- **LISTENING PRACTICE**
  Recent research highlights the importance of helping students at all levels understand authentic spoken English. New as well as revised exercises introduce students to relaxed, reduced speech. The student text audio is available on Essential Online Resources, and a full audio script can be found in the back of the book.

- **READINGS**

  This fourth edition now has a wide selection of readings for students to read and respond to. The content is carefully controlled so that the vocabulary is accessible to beginning students and the grammar structures appropriate to the chapter(s) studied.

- **WRITING TASKS**

  New writing tasks help students naturally produce the target grammar structures in extended discourse. These end-of-chapter activities include writing models for students to follow. Editing checklists draw students' attention to the grammar focus and help them develop proofreading skills.

Components of Basic English Grammar, Fourth Edition:

- **Student Book with Essential Online Resources** includes the access code for the audio, video, self-assessments, and teacher resources with the Student Book answer key.
- **Student Book with MyEnglishLab** that includes the access code to MyEnglishLab, an easy-to-use online learning management system that delivers rich online practice to engage and motivate students.
- A comprehensive *Workbook*, consisting of self-study exercises for independent work.
- An all-new *Teacher's Guide*, with step-by-step teaching suggestions for each chart, notes to the teacher on key grammar structures, vocabulary lists, and expansion activities.
- An expanded *Test Bank*, with additional quizzes, chapter tests, mid-terms, and final exams.
- *ExamView* software that allows teachers to customize their own tests using quizzes and tests from the *Test Bank*.
- *AzarGrammar.com*, a website that provides a variety of supplementary classroom materials, *PowerPoint* presentations for all chapters, and a place where teachers can support each other by sharing their knowledge and experience.

The Student Book answer key is available in the Teacher Resource Folder on Essential Online Resources. Teachers can choose to make the answer key available to their students. Homework can be corrected as a class or, if appropriate, students can correct it at home with the answer key and bring questions to class. In some cases, the teacher may want to collect the assignments written on a separate piece of paper, correct them, and then highlight common problems in class.

MyEnglishLab

MyEnglishLab provides a range of interactive activities that help motivate and engage students. MyEnglishLab for *Basic English Grammar,* Fourth Edition includes:

- Rich online practice for all skill areas: grammar, reading, writing, speaking, and listening
- Instant feedback on incorrect answers
- Remediation activities
- Grammar Coach videos
- Robust assessments that include diagnostic tests, chapter review tests, mid- and end-of-term review tests, and final exams
- Gradebook and diagnostic tools that allow teachers to monitor student progress and analyze data to determine steps for remediation and support
- Student Book answer key in the Teacher Resource Folder

The Azar-Hagen Grammar Series consists of

- *Understanding and Using English Grammar* (blue cover), for upper-level students.
- *Fundamentals of English Grammar* (black cover), for mid-level students.
- *Basic English Grammar* (red cover), for lower or beginning levels.

Tips for Using the New Features in this Text

WARM-UPS

The **Warm-Up** exercises are a brief pre-teaching tool for the charts. They highlight the key point(s) that will be introduced in the chart directly following the **Warm-Up** exercise. Before beginning the task, teachers will want to familiarize themselves with the material in the chart. Then, with the teacher's guidance, students can discover many or all of the new patterns while completing the **Warm-Up** activity. After students finish the exercise, teachers may find that no further explanation is necessary, and the charts can then serve as a useful reference.

LISTENING

The **Listening** exercises have been designed to help students understand American English as it is actually spoken. As such, they include reductions and other phenomena that are part of the natural, relaxed speech of everyday English. Because the pace of speech in the audio may be faster than what students are used to, they may need to hear sentences two or three times as they complete a task.

The **Listening** exercises do not encourage immediate pronunciation (unless they are linked to a specific pronunciation task). Receptive skills precede productive ones, and it is essential that students gain receptive familiarity with the speech patterns before they begin using them in their own speech.

Students are encouraged to listen to conversations the first time without looking at their text. Teachers can explain any vocabulary that has not already been clarified. During the second listening, students complete the assigned task. Teachers will want to pause the audio appropriately. Depending on the level of the class, pauses may be needed after every sentence, or even within a sentence.

It is inevitable that sound representations in the text will at times differ from the instructor's speech, whether due to register or regional variation. A general guideline is that if the instructor expects students will *hear* a variation, or if students themselves raise questions, alternate representations can be presented.

A **Listening Script** is included in the back of the book.

READING

The **Readings** give students an opportunity to work with the grammar structures in extended contexts. Vocabulary that may be new to students is presented on yellow notes for teachers to introduce. One approach to the reading is to have students read the passage independently the first time through. Then they work in small groups or as a class to clarify vocabulary questions that didn't come up in the notes. A second reading may be necessary. Varied reading tasks allow students to check their comprehension, use the target structures, and expand upon the topic in speaking or writing.

WRITING

As students gain confidence in using the target structures, they are encouraged to express their ideas in longer writing tasks. Model paragraphs accompany assignments, and question-prompts help students develop their ideas.

Editing checklists provide guidance for self- or peer-editing. One suggested technique is to pair students, have them exchange papers, and then have the *partner* read the paragraph aloud. The writer can *hear* if the content is what he or she intended. This also keeps the writer from automatically self-correcting while reading aloud. The partner can then offer comments and complete the checklist.

For classes that have not had much experience with writing, the teacher may want students to complete the task in small groups. The group composes a paragraph together, which the teacher then collects and marks by calling attention to beginning-level errors, but not correcting them. The teacher makes a copy for each group member, and each student makes the corrections *individually*.

Let's Talk

Each *Let's Talk* activity is set up as one of the following: **Pairwork**, **Small Group**, **Class Activity**, **Interview**, or **Game**. Language learning is a social activity, and these tasks encourage students to speak with others about their ideas, their everyday lives, and the world around them. Students speak more easily and freely when they can connect language to their own knowledge and experiences.

Check Your Knowledge

Toward the end of the chapter, students can practice sentence-level editing skills by correcting errors common to this level. They can work on the sentences for homework or in small groups in class.

This task can easily be set up as a game. The teacher calls out an item number at random. Students work in teams to correct the sentence, and the first team to correctly edit it wins a point.

Please see the *Teacher's Guide* for detailed information about teaching from this book, including expansion activities and step-by-step instructions.

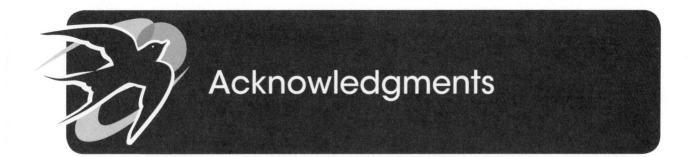

Acknowledgments

Our revision began with extensive reviews from many talented professionals. We are grateful for the expertise of the following teachers: Susan Boland, Tidewater Community College; Lee Chen, Palomar College; Gene Hahn, University of Wisconsin, Stevens Point; Kathleen Keeble, Illinois Institute of Art, Chicago; Steven Lasswell, Santa Barbara City College; Michael Pitts, Los Angeles Southwest College; Carla Reible, Riverside City College; Alison Rice, Hunter College; Maria S. Roche, Housatonic Community College; Nelky Rodriguez, Riverside Community College; John Stasinopoulos, College of DuPage; Hallie Wallack, International Language Institute; Robert L. Woods, Central Washington University.

We were assisted throughout the process by a skilled and dedicated editorial staff. We would like to thank Shelley Hartle, managing editor, for her passion for the series and gifted editing and layout skills; Amy McCormick, editorial director, for guiding the project with exceptional judgment, attentiveness, and foresight; Marian Wassner, senior development editor (and grammar master), for her superb editing and thoughtful responses; Robert Ruvo, production manager, for his deft project management, keen eye for design, and unfailing good humor; Janice Baillie, copy-editor, for her stellar editing and remarkable ability to track all manner of detail; Sue Van Etten, business and website manager, for her expert and dedicated counsel.

We'd also like to express our appreciation to the writers of the supplementary texts: Kelly Roberts Weibel, *Test Bank* and Martha Hall, *Teacher's Guide*. Their creative and fresh ideas greatly enrich the series.

Finally, our thanks to our committed leadership team at Pearson Education who oversaw the entire revision: Pietro Alongi, Rhea Banker, and Paula Van Ells.

We are grateful for the artistic talents of Don Martinetti and Chris Pavely — their colorful work brightens every chapter.

Our families, as always, support and encourage our work. They truly inspire us every day.

Betty S. Azar
Stacy A. Hagen

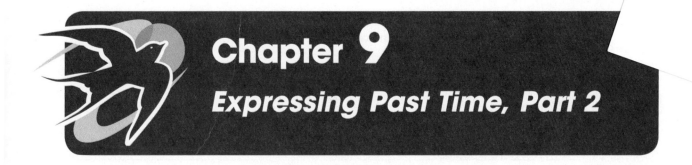

Chapter 9
Expressing Past Time, Part 2

❑ **Exercise 1. Warm-up.** (Chart 9-1)
Choose the correct answer for each question.

1. When did you get to school?
   a. Yes, I did.   b. Downtown.   c. At 11:00.

2. Where were you born?
   a. At midnight.   b. In this city.   c. Yes, I was.

9-1 Simple Past Tense: Using *Where, Why, When,* and *What Time*

QUESTION						SHORT ANSWER
(a)		*Did*	you	*go*	downtown?	→	Yes, I did. / No, I didn't.
(b)	*Where*	*did*	you	*go?*		→	*Downtown.*
(c)		Were	you		downtown?	→	Yes, I was. / No, I wasn't.
(d)	*Where*	were	you?			→	*Downtown.*
(e)		*Did*	you	*run*	because you were late?	→	Yes, I did. / No, I didn't.
(f)	*Why*	*did*	you	*run?*		→	*Because I was late.*
	Why	*didn't*	you	*walk?*			*Because I was late.*
(g)		*Did*	Ann	*come*	at six?	→	Yes, she did. / No, she didn't.
(h)	*When* / *What time*	*did*	Ann	*come?*		→	*At six.*

COMPARE	
(i) *What time* did Ann come? → *At six.* → *Seven o'clock.* → *Around 9:30.*	*What time* usually asks for a specific time on a clock.
(j) *When* did Ann come? → *At six.* → *Friday.* → *June 15th.* → *Last week.* → *Three days ago.*	The answer to *when* can be various expressions of time.

□ **Exercise 2. Looking at grammar.** (Chart 9-1)
Make simple past tense questions and answers about Rosa's vacation.

1. Where . . . go?
2. Why . . . go there?
3. When/What time . . . leave?

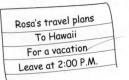

Rosa's travel plans
To Hawaii
For a vacation
Leave at 2:00 P.M.

1. A: _____*Where did Rosa go?*_____
   B: _____*She went to Hawaii.*_____

2. A: _Whe did she go theat ?_
   B: She ____ a ____ a Vacation

3. A: When did she leave?
   B: at 2:00 PM

□ **Exercise 3. Looking at grammar.** (Chart 9-1)
Make questions. Use *where, when, what time,* or *why*.

1. A: _____*Where did you go yesterday?*_____
   B: To the beach. (I went to the beach yesterday.)

2. A: When did Mr. Chu. arrived in Canada
   B: Last month. (Mr. Chu arrived in Canada last month.)

3. A: What time did the Plane arrive ?
   B: At 7:05. (Their plane arrived at 7:05.)

4. A: Why did you stay home last night
   B: Because I was tired. (I stayed home last night because I was tired.)

5. A: Why were you tired last night
   B: Because I stayed up the night before. (I was tired because I stayed up the night before.)

6. A: Why did Sofia go for her vacation?
   B: To Greece. (Sofia went to Greece for her vacation.)

7. A: When did lia finish her homework?
   B: Around midnight. (Lia finished her homework around midnight.)

8. A: When did you come to the city?
   B: Five weeks ago. (I came to this city five weeks ago.)

❏ **Exercise 4. Let's talk: interview.** (Chart 9-1)
Walk around the room. Ask and answer questions using the simple past tense. Share some of your classmates' answers with the class.

Example: What time \ go to bed \ you \ last night?
STUDENT A: What time did you go to bed last night?
STUDENT B: I went to bed at 10:00 last night.

1. What time \ get up \ you \ this morning?
2. When \ finish \ you \ your homework \ last night?
3. Where \ be \ you \ at 10:00 last night?
4. Why \ choose \ you \ this school?
5. Why \ decide \ you \ to study English?
6. What time \ cook \ you \ dinner ?
7. Where \ cook \ you \ dinner?
8. What time \ walk \ you \ into this room?
9. Where \ buy \ you \ this book?
10. When \ buy \ you \ this book?

[handwritten: Where were you be at 10:00 last night? Why did you choose this school? Why did you decide to study english?]

❏ **Exercise 5. Listening.** (Chart 9-1)
Choose the correct answer for each question you hear. Use the information on the datebook pages.

Example: You will hear: Where did Isabel go?
You will choose: a. At 1:00 P.M.   (b.) To the gym.   c. For an exercise class.

Marco's Day		Sabrina's Day		Bill's Day		Isabel's Day	
Mon.	April 4	Mon.	April 4	Mon.	April 4	Mon.	April 4
7:00 A.M.		12:00 Noon		10:00 A.M.		1:00 P.M.	
School		City Café		Dentist		Gym	
meeting with teacher		business meeting		check-up		exercise class	

1. a. At noon.   b. To the City Café.   c. Because she had a meeting.
2. a. At noon.   b. To the City Café.   c. Because she had a meeting.
3. a. To the gym.   b. For an exercise class. c. At 1:00 P.M.
4. a. To the gym.   b. For an exercise class. c. At 1:00 P.M.
5. a. To the gym.   b. For an exercise class. c. At 1:00 P.M.
6. a. Because he had a meeting. b. At 7:00 A.M.   c. To school.
7. a. Because he had a meeting. b. At 7:00 A.M.   c. To school.
8. a. To the dentist.   b. For a check-up.   c. At 10:00 A.M.
9. a. To the dentist.   b. For a check-up.   c. At 10:00 A.M.

❏ **Exercise 6. Looking at grammar.** (Chart 9-1)

Complete the negative questions.

1. A: I didn't go to class yesterday.

   B: Why didn't ___*you go to class*___?

   A: Because I was sick.

2. A: I didn't finish my homework.

   B: Why didn't ___you finish___?

   A: Because I didn't have enough time.

3. A: I didn't eat breakfast this morning.

   B: Why didn't ___you eat breakfast___?

   A: Because I wasn't hungry.

4. A: I didn't clean my apartment last week.

   B: Why didn't ___you clean___?

   A: Because I was too tired.

5. A: I didn't turn on my cell phone yesterday.

   B: Why didn't ___you turn your cell phone on yesterday___?

   A: Because I wanted to finish my work.

❏ **Exercise 7. Listening.** (Chart 9-1)

Listen to the questions. Choose the verb you hear: ***did*** or ***didn't***. *Note:* ***Did you*** can sound like "Did-ja." ***Did he*** can sound like "Dih-de."

Example: You will hear: Why didn't he help?

You will choose: did (didn't)

1. did	didn't	5. did didn't
2. did	didn't	6. did didn't
3. did	didn't	7. did didn't
4. did	didn't	8. did didn't

❏ **Exercise 8. Warm-up.** (Chart 9-2)

Choose the correct answer.

What did you want?

a. Some help. b. Yes, I did. c. Yes, I was. d. Mr. Harris.

9-2 Questions with *What*

What is used in a question when you want to find out about a thing. *Who* is used when you want to find out about a person. (See Chart 9-3 for questions with *Who*.)

(QUESTION + HELPING + SUBJECT + MAIN WORD) VERB VERB					SHORT ANSWER	(LONG ANSWER)
(a)		*Did*	Carol	*buy*	a car? → Yes, she did.	(*She bought a car.*)
(b)	*What*	*did*	Carol	*buy*?	→ *A car.*	(*She bought a car.*)
(c)		*Is*	Fred	*holding*	a book? → Yes, he is.	(*He's holding a book.*)
(d)	*What*	*is*	Fred	*holding*?	→ *A book.*	(*He's holding a book.*)

S V O (e) Carol bought *a car*.	In (e): *a car* is the object of the verb.
O V S V (f) *What* did Carol buy?	In (f): *What* is the object of the verb.

❏ **Exercise 9. Looking at grammar.** (Chart 9-2)
Make questions.

1. A: _____Did you buy a new TV?_____

   B: Yes, I did. (I bought a new TV.)

2. A: _____What did you buy?_____

   B: A new TV. (I bought a new TV.)

3. A: Is Maya crarrying a suitcase_____

   B: Yes, she is. (Maya is carrying a suitcase.)

4. A: What is Maya_____

   B: A suitcase. (Maya is carrying a suitcase.)

5. A: _____

   B: Yes, I do. (I see a plane.)

6. A: _____

   B: A plane. (I see a plane.)

7. A: _____

   B: No, I'm not. (I'm not afraid of mice.) Are you?

8. A: _____

   B: The map on the wall. (The teacher is talking about the map on the wall.)

9. A: _____

   B: Some soup. (Franco had some soup for lunch.)

10. A: <u>Did franco have some soup for lunch?</u>

    B: Yes, he did. (Franco had some soup for lunch.)

11. A: <u>What dose franco usually eat for lunch</u>

    B: A sandwich. (Franco usually eats a sandwich for lunch.)

12. A: <u>Dose franco like Salads</u>

    B: No, he doesn't. (Franco doesn't like salads.)

❏ **Exercise 10. Let's talk: class activity.** (Chart 9-2)
Answer the questions your teacher asks you. Pronounce the verb endings clearly. Close your book for this activity.

Example: walk to the front of the room
  TEACHER: (*Student A*), walk to the front of the room.
STUDENT A: (*walks to the front of the room*)
  TEACHER: (*to Student B*) What did (*Student A*) do?
STUDENT B: She/He walked to the front of the room.
  TEACHER: (*to Student A*) What did you do?
STUDENT A: I walked to the front of the room.

1. smiled
2. laugh
3. cough
4. sneeze
5. shave (*act out*)
6. erase the board
7. sign your name
8. open the door
9. close the door
10. ask a question

11. wash your hands (*act out*)
12. touch the floor
13. point at the door
14. fold a piece of paper
15. count your fingers
16. push (*something in the room*)
17. pull (*something in the room*)
18. yawn
19. pick up your pen
20. add two and two on the board

❏ **Exercise 11. Vocabulary and grammar.** (Chart 9-2)
Ask your teacher for the meaning of the given words. Begin your question with **What**.

Example: century
STUDENT: What does *century* mean?
TEACHER: *Century* means "100 years."

1. humid رطب
2. awful مريع
3. quiet هادئ

4. grocery store
5. pretty difficult
6. ill

7. murder
8. enjoy
9. old-fashioned

❏ **Exercise 12. Let's talk: class activity.** (Charts 9-1 and 9-2)
Ask your teacher questions to complete the chart with information about each person's day.★

SITUATION: All these women were absent from school yesterday. What did each person do? In your opinion, who had the best day? أدي

Example:
STUDENT A: What time did Jenny wake up?
  TEACHER: 7:00 A.M.
STUDENT B: What did Jin eat for breakfast?
  TEACHER: Rice.

	wake up	eat for breakfast	spend the day	go to bed	absent غائب
JENNY	7:00 A.M.				
JIN		rice			
JADA			at the beach		
JANICE				10:00 P.M.	
JULIANNA					Because she needed to earn extra money for school tuition.

❏ **Exercise 13. Listening.** (Charts 9-1 and 9-2)
Listen to the questions. Write the words you hear.

Example: You will hear: Where did they go?
    You will write: ___*Where did they*___ go?

1. ___When di did you___ arrive?
2. ___Why did you___ leave?
3. ___What did she want___ want?
4. ___Where did you study___ study?

5. ___What did he say___ say?
6. ___When did they___ move?
7. ___Where did they___ move to?

★*Teacher:* See Let's Talk: Answers, p. 503.

❏ **Exercise 14. Warm-up.** (Chart 9-3)

Match each picture with the correct conversation.

Picture A

Picture B

1. A: Who did you pick up at the airport?
   B: My father.

2. A: Who picked you up at the airport?
   B: My father.

9-3 Questions with *Who* and *Whom*

	QUESTION	ANSWER	
(a)	*What* did they see? → *A boat.* (*They saw a boat.*)		*What* is used to ask questions about *things.*
(b)	*Who* did they see? → *Jay.* (*They saw Jay.*)		*Who* is used to ask questions about *people.*
(c)	*Who* did they see? → *Jay.* (*They saw Jay.*)		Examples (c) and (d) have the same meaning.
(d)	*Whom* did they see? → *Jay.* (*They saw Jay.*)		*Whom* is used in formal English as the object of a verb or a preposition.
			In (c): *Who*, not *whom*, is usually used in everyday English.
			In (d): *Whom* is used in very formal English. *Whom* is rarely used in everyday spoken English.

	QUESTION	ANSWER	
(e)	ᵒ *Who(m)* did they see? →	ᵒ *Jay.* (*They saw Jay.*)	In (e): *Who(m)* is the object of the verb. Usual question word order is used: *question word + helping verb + subject + main verb*
(f)	ˢ *Who* saw Jay? →	ˢ *Ella.* (*Ella saw Jay.*)	In (f), (g), and (h): *Who* is the subject of the question. Usual question word order is NOT used. When *who* is the subject of a
(g)	ˢ *Who* lives there? →	ˢ *Ed.* (*Ed lives there.*)	question, do NOT use *does, do,* or *did.* Do NOT change the verb in any way: the verb
(h)	ˢ *Who* came? →	ˢ *Eva.* (*Eva came.*)	form in the question is the same as the verb form in the answer.
	INCORRECT: *Who did come?*		

❏ **Exercise 15. Looking at grammar.** (Chart 9-3)
Work with a partner. Make questions orally with *who*. Then write the questions.

Example: The teacher saw Alan. The teacher talked to Alan. The teacher helped Alan.

→ a. _____Who saw Alan_____? The teacher.
→ b. _____Who talked to Alan_____? The teacher.
→ c. _____Who helped Alan_____? The teacher.
→ d. _____Who did the teacher see_____? Alan.
→ e. _____Who did the teacher talk to_____? Alan.
→ f. _____Who did the teacher help_____? Alan.

1. Alan called Yuko. Alan visited Yuko. Alan studied with Yuko.

a. _____Who called Yuko_____? Alan.

أذا كان في السؤال فاعل

b. _____Who visited Yuko_____? Alan.

يكون فيرب عادي بدون Ed

c. _____Who Studied Yuko_____? Alan.

d. _____? Yuko.

e. _____? Yuko.

f. _____Who did Alms_____? Yuko.

بدون

Alan عشان يحافظ

2. Ron talked to the kids. Ron watched the kids. Ron played with the kids.

a. _____? Ron.

b. _____? The kids.

c. _____? Ron.

d. _____? The kids.

e. _____? Ron.

f. _____? The kids.

❏ **Exercise 16. Looking at grammar.** (Chart 9-3)
Make questions. Answer the questions where necessary.

1. Astrid carried the baby.

a. Who carried _____the baby_____? Astrid.

b. Who did _____carry_____? The baby.

2. The firefighter saved the woman.

    a. Who did _the firefighter_? The woman.

    b. Who saved _the woman_? The firefighter.

3. Professor Ramic taught the students.

    a. Who taught _____? _____.

    b. Who did _____? _____.

❏ **Exercise 17. Looking at grammar.** (Chart 9-3)
Make questions.

    1. A: _____

       B: Nina. (I saw Nina at the party.)

    2. A: _____

       B: Nina. (Nina came to the party.)

    3. A: _____

       B: Kenji. (I talked to Kenji.)

    4. A: _____

       B: Abbey. (Barak helped Abbey.)

    5. A: _____

       B: Barak. (Barak helped Abbey.)

    6. A: _____

       B: Barak and Abbey. (I invited Barak and Abbey.)

❑ **Exercise 18. Let's talk: pairwork.** (Charts 9-1 → 9-3)
Work with a partner. Finish this conversation between a parent and a teenager. Use your imagination. You can make it funny or serious. Perform your conversation for the class.

PARENT: Where did you go last night?

TEENAGER: _____
                                        1

PARENT: What did you do?

TEENAGER: _____
                                        2

PARENT: Who did you see?

TEENAGER: _____
                                        3

PARENT: Who saw you?

TEENAGER: _____
                                        4

PARENT: When did you get home?

TEENAGER: _____
                                        5

PARENT: Is there anything else you want to tell me?

TEENAGER: _____
                                        6

PARENT: You're grounded!*

---

to be grounded: a type of punishment from a parent: the child stays at home and can't do activities with friends.

❏ **Exercise 19. Listening.** (Charts 9-1 → 9-3)

Listen to each question and choose the best answer.

Example: You will hear: Why was John late?
You will choose: a. Yesterday.   b. At the park.   ⓒ Because he slept too long.

1. a. At midnight.
   b. Because it was late.
   c. With my parents.

2. a. Last month.
   b. In a small town.
   c. Because he was a co-worker.

3. a. In a minute.
   b. Some money.
   c. John and Sarah.

4. a. At work.
   b. At 10:00.
   c. There was a party.

5. a. An apartment downtown.
   b. Next week.
   c. Because we like the city.

6. a. The bus.
   b. Because her car didn't start.
   c. Maya did.

7. a. Because I didn't have time.
   b. My friends.
   c. It was fun.

❏ **Exercise 20. Game.** (Chart 9-3)

Work in teams. Choose two places from the list and write as many questions as you can for each situation. Try to use a mix of *Wh*-questions: **When, Where, What time, Who,** and **Why.** The team with the most grammatically correct questions wins.

Example: Your friend just got home from the shopping mall.
Possible questions: What did you buy? Where did you shop? Etc.

Your friend just got home from . . .

1. the shopping mall.
2. the library.
3. the airport.

4. the dentist's office.
5. the train station.
6. the movies.

7. the hospital.
8. a one-week vacation.
9. a soccer tournament.

❏ **Exercise 21. Warm-up.** (Chart 9-4)

Complete the sentences with your own words.

1. a. Right now a pack of gum costs _____.

   b. When I was a child, a pack of gum cost _____.

2. a. In restaurants, some chefs make _____ for dinner.

   b. The last time I cooked dinner, I made _____.

9-4 Simple Past Tense: Irregular Verbs (Group 5)

cost – cost	hit – hit	shut – shut
cut – cut	hurt – hurt	spend – spent
forget – forgot	lend – lent	understand – understood
give – gave	make – made	

❑ **Exercise 22. Vocabulary and speaking.** (Chart 9-4)

Practice using irregular verbs. Close your book for this activity.

Example: **cost–cost**

TEACHER: cost–cost. Gasoline costs a lot of money. Yesterday, I bought gas for my car.
It cost a lot of money. How much did it cost?
STUDENTS: (*repeat*) cost–cost. It cost a lot of money.

1. **cost–cost** I bought a jacket yesterday. I paid a lot for it. It cost (. . .). What did I buy yesterday? How much did it cost?

2. **cut–cut** (. . .) cuts vegetables when he/she makes a salad. Two nights ago, he/she made a salad and cut his/her finger with the knife. What happened two nights ago?

3. **forget–forgot** Sometimes I forget my wallet. Last night, I forgot it at a restaurant. What did I do last night?

4. **give–gave** People give gifts on birthdays. Last week, (. . .) had a birthday. I gave him/her (*something*). What did I do?

5. **hit–hit** When you play tennis, you hit the ball with a tennis racket. When you play table tennis, you hit the ball with a paddle. What do you do when you play tennis? What do you do when you play table tennis?

6. **hurt–hurt** When I have a headache, my head hurts. Yesterday I had a headache. My head hurt. How did my head feel yesterday? How does your head feel when you have a headache?

7. **lend–lent** I lend money to my friends if they need it. Yesterday I lent (*an amount of money*) to (. . .). What did I do?

8. **make–made** I know how to make ice cream! Last week I made chocolate ice cream for a birthday party. What did I do last week?

9. **shut–shut** I shut the garage door every night at 10:00 P.M. I shut it early last night. What did I do last night?

10. **spend–spent** I usually spend Saturdays with friends. But last Saturday, I spent the day with my parents. What did I do last Saturday?

11. **understand–understood** I don't always understand singers when they sing. But yesterday I listened to a new song, and I understood every word. What did I understand?

❏ **Exercise 23. Looking at grammar.** (Chart 9-4)
Complete each sentence. Use the correct form of the word in parentheses.

1. A: How much does a new car cost?

    B: It (*cost*) _____costs_____ a lot. New cars are expensive.

2. A: Did you get a ticket for the rock concert?

    B: No, it (*cost*) _____ too much.

3. A: Where's your history book?

    B: I (*give*) _____ it to Robert.

4. A: What happened?

    B: I had a car accident. I (*hit*) _____
    a telephone pole.

5. A: May I have your homework, please?

    B: I'm sorry, but I don't have it. I (*forget*) _____ it.

6. A: Did you eat breakfast?

    B: Yeah. I (*make*) _____ some scrambled eggs and toast for myself.

7. Eric (*shut*) _____ the window when he wakes up every morning.

8. Eric (*shut*) _____ the window when he woke up yesterday morning.

9. A: Did you enjoy going into the city to see a show?

    B: Yes, but I (*spend*) _____ a lot of money.

10. A: Do you have a calculator?

    B: Yes, but I (*lend*) _____ it to George.

11. A: Is that knife sharp?

    B: It's very sharp. It (*cut*) _____ everything easily.

12. A: Why are you wearing a cap on your head? It's so hot today.

    B: I went to a barber this morning. He (*cut*) _____ my hair too short.

    A: Let me see. Oh, it looks fine.

❑ **Exercise 24. Listening.** (Chart 9-4)

Listen to the beginning of each sentence. Choose the correct completion(s). There may be more than one correct answer.

Example: You will hear: Kurt made . . .

You will choose: (a.) his lunch.   (b.) furniture.   c. in the morning.

1. a. the answer.   b. the conversation.   c. the teacher.

2. a. money.   b. to her house.   c. some furniture.

3. a. your hair?   b. some paper?   c. between?

4. a. tomorrow.   b. a tree.   c. an animal.

5. a. remember.   b. his appointment.   c. the question.

❑ **Exercise 25. Warm-up.** (Chart 9-5)

Which answers are true for you?

1. a. Right now I feel   fine / okay / tired / hungry.

   b. On the first day of class, I felt   fine / okay / nervous / scared.

2. a. My favorite sports team   wins / doesn't win   a lot of games.

   b. My favorite sports team   won / didn't win   its last game.

9-5 Simple Past Tense: Irregular Verbs (Group 6)

blow – blew	grow – grew	swim – swam
draw – drew	keep – kept	throw – threw
fall – fell	know – knew	win – won
feel – felt		

❑ **Exercise 26. Vocabulary and speaking.** (Chart 9-5).

Practice using irregular verbs. Close your book for this activity.

Example: ***fall–fell***

TEACHER: fall–fell. Rain falls. Leaves fall. Sometimes people fall. Yesterday I fell down. I hurt my knee. How did I hurt my knee yesterday?

STUDENTS: (*repeat*) fall–fell. You fell (down).

1. ***blow–blew***   The sun shines. Rain falls. Wind blows. Last week we had a storm. It rained hard, and the wind blew hard. Tell me about the storm last week.

2. **draw–drew** I draw once a week in art class. Last week I drew a picture of a mountain. What did I do in art class last week?

3. **fall–fell** Sometimes I fall down. Yesterday I fell down some steps outside my house. What happened to me yesterday?

4. **feel–felt** Sometimes I feel sleepy in class. I felt tired all day yesterday. How did I feel yesterday? How did you feel yesterday?

5. **grow–grew** Trees grow. Flowers grow. Vegetables grow. Usually I grow vegetables in my garden, but last year I grew only flowers. What did I grow in my garden last year?

6. **keep–kept** Now I keep my money in (*name of a local bank*). Last year I kept my money in (*name of another local bank*). Where did I keep my money last year?

7. **know–knew** This class knows a lot about English grammar. Last week, many students knew the answers to my questions. What did many students know last week?

8. **swim–swam** I swim in (*name of a lake, sea, ocean, or local swimming pool*) every summer. I swam in (*name of a lake, sea, ocean, or local swimming pool*) last summer. What did I do last summer?

9. **throw–threw** In baseball, the pitcher throws the ball. I like to play baseball. I like to throw the ball. Yesterday, when I played baseball, I was the pitcher. What did I do with the ball?

a pitcher

a batter

10. **win–won** You can win a game or lose a game. Last weekend (*name of a local sports team*) won a game/match against (*name of another team*). What did (*name of the local sports team*) do last weekend? Did they win or lose?

❏ **Exercise 27. Looking at grammar.** (Chart 9-5)
Complete the sentences. Use the simple past form of the verbs from the box.

blow	fall	grow	know	throw
draw	feel	keep	swim	win

1. A: Did you enjoy your tennis game with Jackie?

   B: Yes, but I lost. Jackie _____.

2. A: How did you break your leg?

   B: I _____ down on the ice on the sidewalk.

3. A: Did you give the box of candy to your girlfriend?

   B: No, I didn't. I _____ it and ate it myself.

4. A: That's a nice picture.

   B: I agree. Tanya _____ it. She's a good artist.

5. A: Your daughter is so tall!

   B: I know. She _____ a lot last year.

6. A: I burned my finger.

   B: Did you put ice on it?

   A: No. I _____ on it.

7. A: Did you finish the test?

   B: No. I _____ all of the answers, but I ran out of time.

8. A: Did you have fun at the beach?

   B: Lots of fun. We _____ in the ocean.

9. A: What's the matter? You sound like you have a frog in your throat.

   B: I think I'm catching a cold. I _____ okay yesterday, but I don't feel very good today.

10. A: How did you break the window, Tommy?

    B: Well, I _____ a ball to Julie, but it missed Julie and hit the window instead.

❑ **Exercise 28. Listening.** (Chart 9-5)

Listen to the beginning of each sentence. Choose the correct completion(s). There may be more than one correct answer.

Example: You will hear: Tim knew . . .
        You will choose: (a.) my father.   b. a ball.   (c.) the answer.

1. a. tomorrow.   b. on a car.   c. in the park.

2. a. the game.   b. a prize.   c. lost.

3. a. on the paper.   b. a picture.   c. with a pencil.

4. a. happy.   b. in the morning.   c. excited.

5. a. a ball.   b. not.   c. a pillow.

❑ **Exercise 29. Warm-up.** (Chart 9-6)

Make true sentences for you.

1. Some people feed animals at the zoo.

   When I was a child, I   fed / didn't feed   animals at the zoo.

2. During storms, some kids hide in closets or under the bed.

   When I was a child, I   hid / didn't hide   during a storm.

9-6 Simple Past Tense: Irregular Verbs (Group 7)

become – became	build – built	hide – hid
bend – bent	feed – fed	hold – held
bite – bit	fight – fought	shake – shook

❏ **Exercise 30. Vocabulary and speaking.** (Chart 9-6)

Practice using irregular verbs. Close your book for this activity.

Example: **hold–held**

TEACHER: hold–held. I often hold my book open when I teach. Yesterday I held my book open when we practiced grammar. What did I do with my book?
STUDENTS: (*repeat*) hold–held. You held your book open.

1. ***become–became*** Lilly got the flu last month. She became very sick. Now she is better. What happened when Lilly got the flu?

2. ***bend–bent*** When I drop something, I bend over to pick it up. I just dropped my pen, and then I bent over to pick it up. What did I do?

3. ***bite–bit*** Sometimes dogs bite people. Yesterday my friend's dog bit my hand when I petted it. What did the dog do?

4. ***build–built*** I have some friends who know how to build houses. They built their own house next to the river. What did my friends do?

5. ***feed–fed*** I have a (dog, cat, parrot, etc.). I have to feed it every day. Yesterday I fed it once in the morning and once in the evening. What did I do yesterday?

6. ***fight–fought*** People fight in wars. People fight diseases. They fight for freedom. My country fought a war in (*year*). What did my country do in (*year*)?

7. ***hide–hid*** I have a coin in my hand. Close your eyes while I hide it. Okay, open your eyes. I hid the coin. Where's the coin? Why don't you know?

8. ***hold–held*** When it rains, I hold my umbrella above my head. Yesterday it rained. I held my umbrella above my head. What did I do yesterday?

9. ***shake–shook*** People sometimes shake their finger or their head. Sometimes they shake when they're cold. Right now I'm shaking my (finger/head). What did I just do?

❏ **Exercise 31. Looking at grammar.** (Chart 9-6).

Complete the sentences. Use the past simple form of the verbs from the box.

become	build	hide
bend	feed	hold
bite	fight	shake

1. Many countries in the world _____*fought*_____ in World War II.

2. I need a new pair of glasses. I sat on my old glasses and

_____ them.

3. I _____ my husband's birthday present in the

closet yesterday. I didn't want him to find it.

4. Emma and Steve saved money. They didn't buy a bookcase for their new apartment.

They bought wood and _____ one.

5. The baby is sleeping peacefully. She's not hungry. Her mother _____

her before she put her in bed.

6. David is a Canadian citizen. Maria was born in Puerto Rico, but when she married

David, she _____ a Canadian citizen too.

7. Doug is a new father. He felt very happy when he _____ his baby in his

arms for the first time.

8. A: Ouch!

   B: What's the matter?

   A: I _____ my tongue.

9. When my dog got out of the lake, it _____

itself. Dogs always do that when they're wet.

❑ **Exercise 32. Listening.** (Chart 9-6)

Listen to the beginning of each sentence. Choose the correct completion(s). There may be more than one correct answer.

Example: You will hear: I bent . . .

  You will choose: ⓐ my arm.   b. a building.   c. the road.

1. a. the dog.   b. happy.   c. her baby.
2. a. next week.   b. usually.   c. a new house.
3. a. a stick.   b. my hand.   c. sad.
4. a. in the bedroom.   b. behind a tree.   c. their money.
5. a. some pens.   b. the classroom.   c. some papers.

❏ **Exercise 33. Warm-up.** (Chart 9-7)
Which completions are true for you?

1. *Before I ate breakfast this morning, I . . .*
   a. took a shower.
   b. washed my face.
   c. made tea.
   d. combed my hair.

2. *After I got to school today, I . . .*
   a. ate something.
   b. bought some coffee.
   c. did my homework.
   d. talked to friends.

9-7 *Before* and *After* in Time Clauses

(a) S V *I ate breakfast.* = a main clause	A clause is a group of words that has a subject and a verb.
(b) S V ***before*** *I went to class* = a time clause (c) S V I ate breakfast │ ***before*** *I went to class.* main clause time clause	A main clause is a complete sentence. Example (a) is a complete sentence. Example (b) is an incomplete sentence. It must be connected to a main clause, as in (c) and (d).

(d) S V
Before *I went to class,* │ I ate breakfast.
   time clause   main clause
	A time clause begins with a time word such as ***before*** or ***after***:
	   before + S + V = a time clause
	   after + S + V = a time clause

(e) We took a walk │ ***after*** *we finished our work.*
   main clause   time clause
 	
(f) ***After*** *we finished our work,* │ we took a walk.
   time clause   main clause
	A time clause can come after a main clause, as in (c) and (e). A time clause can come before a main clause, as in (d) and (f).* There is no difference in meaning between (c) and (d) or between (e) and (f).

(g) We took a walk │ *after the movie.*
            prep. phrase
 	
(h) I had a cup of coffee │ *before class.*
            prep. phrase
	Before and ***after*** don't always introduce a time clause. They are also used as prepositions followed by a noun object, as in (g) and (h). See Charts 1-8, p. 21, and 6-2, p. 161, for information about prepositional phrases.

* NOTE: When a time clause comes before the main clause, a comma is used between the two clauses. A comma is not used when the time clause comes after the main clause.

❏ **Exercise 34. Looking at grammar.** (Chart 9-7)
Put brackets around the main clause and the time clause in each sentence. Write "M" over the main clause and "T" over the time clause.

         T   M
1. [Before I ate the banana,] [I peeled it.]

          M   T
2. [We arrived at the airport] before the plane landed.

      M T
3. [I went to a movie] after I finished my homework. → after I finished my homework I went to a movie

تقد رباعی / جملة تخلی ووسط

قبل وحدة

4. (After the kids got home from school,) they watched TV.

5. (Before I moved to this city,) I lived at home with my parents.

□ **Exercise 35. Looking at grammar.** (Chart 9-7)
In the first pair of sentences, write "1" before the activity that happens first and "2" before the activity that happens second. Then choose the sentence(s) with the correct meaning.

1. __2__ Salman went to sleep.
   __1__ Salman watched a movie.
   a. Before Salman went to sleep, he watched a movie.
   b. Before Salman watched a movie, he went to sleep.

2. __2__ We went home.
   __1__ We left my uncle's house.
   a. After we went home, we left my uncle's house.
   b. After we left my uncle's house, we went home.

3. __1__ I washed the dishes.
   __2__ I put them away.
   a. After I put the dishes away, I washed them.
   b. Before I put the dishes away, I washed them.

4. __1__ The lions chased the zebra.
   __2__ The lions ate the zebra.
   a. Before the lions ate the zebra, they chased it.
   b. Before the lions chased the zebra, they ate it.
   c. After the lions chased the zebra, they ate it.
   d. After the lions ate the zebra, they chased it.

□ **Exercise 36. Game.** (Chart 9-7)
Work in teams. Find all the incomplete sentences. Make them complete and add the correct punctuation. Your teacher will give you a time limit. The team with the most grammatically correct answers wins.

Example: Before my cell phone died last night
Possible answer: Before my cell phone died last night, I texted several friends.

1. After Jonas and Nora got married in Hawaii last June, they moved to New York.
2. We went to the zoo before we ate our lunch. before they went home
3. The kids played soccer in the park before the went home
4. After you finished your homework last night you watched TV.
5. Vikram didn't eat before he took his medicine.
6. Before I took my daughter to the dentist last week, we visited my mother.
7. After school started at the beginning of the year I made a lot of new friends
8. Before Gino told me about his problems, I thought he was happy.

Work in small groups. Combine the two ideas into one sentence by using **before** and **after** to introduce time clauses. Make four sentences for each item.

Example: I put on my coat. / I went outside.

STUDENT A: Before I went outside, I put on my coat.
STUDENT B: I put on my coat before I went outside.
STUDENT C: After I put on my coat, I went outside.
STUDENT D: I went outside after I put on my coat.

1. She ate breakfast. / She went to work.

2. He did his homework. / He went to bed.

3. We bought tickets. / We walked into the movie theater.

❏ **Exercise 38. Warm-up.** (Chart 9-8)
Do the sentences have the same or a different meaning?

1. When I got home from school, I ate a snack.
2. I ate a snack when I got home from school.

9-8 *When* in Time Clauses

(a) **When** *the rain stopped,* we took a walk. OR We took a walk *when the rain stopped.*	**When** can introduce a time clause. **when** + S + V = a time clause In (a): **When** *the rain stopped* is a time clause.
(b) *When* **Tom** *was a child,* **he** *lived with his aunt.* OR **Tom** *lived with his aunt when* **he** *was a child.*	In (b): Notice that the noun (*Tom*) comes before the pronoun (*he*).
COMPARE (c) *When did the rain stop?* = a question (d) *when the rain stopped* = a time clause	**When** is also used to introduce questions.* A question is a complete sentence, as in (c). A time clause is not a complete sentence, as in (d).

*See Charts 3-11, p. 89, and 9-1 for information about using *when* in questions.

❏ **Exercise 39. Looking at grammar.** (Chart 9-8)
Add a capital letter and a question mark to complete the sentences. Write "NC" to mean "not complete" if the group of words is a time clause and not a question.

1. a. when did Jim arrive → *W̶hen did Jim arrive?*

   b. when Jim arrived → *NC, played soccer*

2. a. when you were in Iran → *NC, visited my family*

   b. when were you in Iran → *When were you in Iran?*

3. a. When did the movie end ?

   b. when the movie ended , *we went to the gym.*

4. a. when Khalid and Bakir were at the restaurant on First Street, *they watched the*
   crime.
   b. When were Khalid and Bakir at the restaurant on First Street ?

5. a. when the museum opens , *they could buy the tickets .*

   b. When does the museum open ?

❑ **Exercise 40. Looking at grammar.** (Chart 9-8)
Make sentences by combining the ideas in Column A with those in Column B. Then change the position of the time clause.

Example: When the show ended,
   → When the show ended, people clapped.
   → People clapped when the show ended.

Column A	Column B
1. When the show ended,	a. when I dropped it.
2. When I was in Japan,	b. I closed my umbrella.
3. Elena bought some new shoes	c. when he was in high school.
4. I took a lot of photographs	d. people clapped.
5. Adam was a soccer player	e. when she went shopping yesterday.
6. When the rain stopped,	f. I stayed in a hotel in Tokyo.
7. The mirror broke	g. when I was in Hawaii.

❑ **Exercise 41. Looking at grammar.** (Chart 9-8)
Use the given words to make (a) a simple past tense question and (b) a simple past tense clause. Use your own words to complete the sentence in (b).

1. When \ snow \ it

   a. _____*When did it snow?*_____

   b. _____*When it snowed, I built a snowman.*_____

I stayed in hotel into

2. When \ leave \ you
   a. _When did you leave?_
   b. _When you left._

3. When \ feel homesick \ Thomas
   a. _When did Thomas feel homesick?_
   b. _Whe Thomas felt, he took the medicines._

4. When \ go out \ electricity
   a. _When did the electricity go out?_
   b. _When the electricity went out, we were hot._

❑ **Exercise 42. Warm-up.** (Chart 9-9)
Complete the sentences with the correct time for you.

1. Now I am studying grammar, but yesterday I wasn't studying grammar at

   _____ .

2. Now I am not sleeping, but last night, I was sleeping at _____ .

9-9 Present Progressive and Past Progressive

PRESENT PROGRESSIVE (in progress right now) (a) It's 10:00 now. Boris *is sitting* in class.	The present progressive describes an activity in progress right now, at the moment of speaking. See Chart 4-1, p. 96. In (a): Right now it is 10:00. Boris began to sit before 10:00. Sitting is in progress at 10:00. (See next page.)
PAST PROGRESSIVE (in progress yesterday) (b) It was 10:00. Boris *was sitting* in class.	The past progressive describes an activity in progress at a particular time in the past. In (b): Boris began to sit in class before 10:00 yesterday. At 10:00 yesterday, sitting in class was in progress. (See next page.)

PRESENT PROGRESSIVE FORM: *AM, IS, ARE* + *-ING*
(c) It's 10:00. I   *am sitting* in class.
         Boris *is sitting* in class.
         We   *are sitting* in class.
	The forms of the present progressive and the past progressive consist of *be* + *-ing*. The present progressive uses the present forms of *be*: *am*, *is*, and *are* + *-ing*.

PAST PROGRESSIVE FORM: *WAS, WERE* + *-ING* (d) It was 10:00. Boris *was sitting* in class. We *were sitting* in class.	The past progressive uses the past forms of *be*: *was* and *were* + *-ing*.

Boris *is sitting* in class right now at ten o'clock.

Boris *was sitting* in class yesterday at ten o'clock.

❑ **Exercise 43. Grammar and speaking: class activity.** (Chart 9-9)
Complete each sentence with the correct form of the verb in parentheses. Discuss the meaning of the phrase "in progress."

1. Paul started to eat dinner at 7:00. At 7:05, Kara came. Paul (*eat*)

_____was eating_____ when Kara (*come*) _____came_____ at 7:05.

2. Bobby was at home yesterday evening. His favorite program was on TV last night. It started at 8:00. It ended at 9:00. At 8:30, his friend Kristin called.

When Kristin (*call*) __called__ at 8:30, Bobby (*watch*) __was watching__ TV.

3. Rosa played her guitar for an hour yesterday morning. She started to play her guitar at 9:30. She stopped at 10:30. Mike arrived at her apartment at 10:00.

At 10:00, Rosa (*play*) __was playing__ her guitar.

Exercise 44. Let's talk: class activity. (Chart 9-9)

Look at the picture. Use the past progressive to describe the activities that were in progress the night of the robbery.

SITUATION: Mr. and Mrs. Gold invited some friends to their house for the weekend. A thief stole Mrs. Gold's jewelry at midnight on Saturday. What were the guests doing at midnight?

❑ **Exercise 45. Warm-up.** (Chart 9-10)

Check (✓) <u>all</u> the sentences that match the picture.

While the teacher was talking,

1. _____ the fire alarm began to ring.

2. _____ a student fell asleep.

3. _____ a spider crawled into the room.

4. _____ a desk fell over.

5. _____ another teacher came into the room.

6. _____ the room caught fire.

9-10 Using *While* with Past Progressive

(a) The phone rang **while** *I was sleeping*. OR	**while** + *subject* + *verb* = *a time clause* *While I was sleeping* is a time clause. *while* = *during that time*
(b) **While** *I was sleeping*, the phone rang.*	A *while*-clause describes an activity that was in progress at the time another activity happened. The verb in a *while*-clause is often past progressive (e.g., *was sleeping*).

*NOTE: When a time clause comes before the main clause, a comma is used between the two clauses. A comma is not used when the time clause comes after the main clause.

❑ **Exercise 46. Let's talk: class activity.** (Chart 9-10)
Combine the sentences. Use *while*.

1. I was studying last night.
   Rita called.
   → *While I was studying last night, Rita called.*
   → *Rita called while I was studying last night.*

2. Someone knocked on my apartment door.
   I was eating breakfast yesterday.
   While I was eating breakfast yesterday, Someone knocked on my apt door.

3. I was cooking dinner last night.
   I burned my hand.
   While I was cooking dinner last night, I burned my hand.

4. Yoko raised her hand.
   The teacher was talking.
   While the teacher was talking, Yoko raised her hand.

5. A tree fell on my car.
   I was driving in a windstorm.
   While I was driving in a windstorm, a tree fell on my car.

6. I was studying last night.
   A mouse suddenly appeared on my desk.
   While I was studying last night, a mouse suddenly appeared on my desk.

❑ **Exercise 47. Warm-up.** (Chart 9-11)
What word begins each time clause? What verb form is in each time clause?

1. a. While I was studying, the mouse appeared.

   b. The mouse appeared while I was studying.

2. a. When the mouse appeared, I was studying.

   b. I was studying when the mouse appeared.

9-11 Simple Past Tense vs. Past Progressive

(a) Jane *called* me yesterday. (b) I *talked* to Jane for an hour last night. (c) What time *did* you *get up* this morning?	The SIMPLE PAST describes activities or situations that began and ended at a particular time in the past (e.g., *yesterday, last night*).
(d) I *was studying* when Jane called me last night. (e) While I *was studying* last night, Jane called.	The PAST PROGRESSIVE describes an activity that was in progress (was happening) at the time another action happened. In (d) and (e): The studying was in progress when Jane called. ***When*** is commonly used with the simple past activity, as in (d).
2 1 (f) | I *opened* my umbrella | | when it *began* to rain. | main clause time clause	If both the time clause and the main clause in a sentence are simple past, it means that the action in the time clause happened first, and the action in the main clause happened second. In (f): First, it began to rain; second, I opened my umbrella.
COMPARE (g) When the phone *rang,* I *answered* it. (h) When the phone *rang,* I *was studying.*	In (g): First, the phone rang; second, I answered it. In (h): First, the studying was in progress; second, the phone rang.

❏ **Exercise 48. Let's talk: class activity.** (Chart 9-11)

Your teacher will ask you to perform and describe actions using *while*-clauses or *when*-clauses. Close your book for this activity.

Example: Erase the board. / Open the door.
 TEACHER: (*Student A*), please erase the board. What are you doing?
 STUDENT A: (*erases the board*) I'm erasing the board right now.
 TEACHER: (*Student B*), would you please open the door?
 STUDENT B: (*opens the door*)
 TEACHER: Thank you. You may both sit down. (*Student C*), will you please describe the two actions we saw?
 STUDENT C: While (*Student A*) was erasing the board, (*Student B*) opened the door. OR (*Student A*) was erasing the board when (*Student B*) opened the door.

1. Write on the board. / Drop a book on the floor.
2. Walk around the room. / Say hello to (*Student A*).
3. Look out the window. / Take (*Student A*)'s grammar book.
4. Draw a picture on the board. / Ask (*Student A*) a question.

❑ **Exercise 49. Looking at grammar.** (Chart 9-11)
Complete the sentences. Use the past progressive in the *while*-clauses. Use the simple past in the *when*-clauses.

1. While I (*wash*) ___was washing___ the dishes last night, I (*get*) _____got_____

   a phone call from my best friend.

2. When my best friend (*call*) _____ last night, I (*wash*) _____

   _____ the dishes.

3. My friend Jessica (*come*) _____ over while I (*eat*) _____

   _____ dinner last night.

4. I (*eat*) _____ dinner when my friend Jessica (*come*)

   _____ over last night.

5. My friend Ricardo (*come*) _____ when I (*stream*) _____

   _____ a movie on my computer last night. I (*invite*)

   _____ him to watch it with me.

6. I (*stream*) _____ a movie on my computer last night when my friend

   Ricardo (*come*) _____ over.

7. Jason (*wear*) _____ a suit and tie when I (*see*) _____

   him yesterday.

8. While I (*watch*) _____ TV in bed last night and (*relax*)

   _____ after a long day, my new puppy (*take*) _____

my slippers.

Part I. Work with a partner. Use the information about Bill Gates to make sentences with the simple past and past progressive. Use *while, when, before,* and *after.*

Example: 1967: entered Lakeside School
1968: wrote his first computer program
→ *In 1967, Bill Gates entered Lakeside School.*
→ *While he was studying at Lakeside, he wrote his first computer program.*

Bill Gates: a brief history

1955:	was born in Seattle, Washington
1967:	entered Lakeside School
1967–1973:	studied at Lakeside School
1968:	wrote his first computer program
1970:	started his first software company
1973:	graduated from Lakeside
1973–1977:	studied at Harvard University
1975:	began to design programs for personal computers
1975:	started Microsoft with Paul Allen
1975–2008:	led Microsoft
1977:	left Harvard University
1994:	got married to Melinda French
1996:	his first child was born
2008:	retired from Microsoft
2008:	became more active in the Bill and Melinda Gates Foundation

Part II. Make a timeline of seven to ten events in your partner's life. Write sentences with the simple past and past progressive. Use *while, when, before,* and *after.*

☐ **Exercise 51. Reading and listening.** (Charts 9-7 → 9-11)
Part I. Read the story about Steve Jobs. Look at new vocabulary with your teacher first.

Steve Jobs

Steve Jobs is another very famous computer person. He was also born in 1955. He grew up in Palo Alto, California. When he was in high school, he worked for electronics businesses in the summer. He also met Steve Wozniak. They became friends and business partners and built their first computer together.

Do you know these words?
electronics
design
fired
cancer
medical treatments
cure
turned + (age)

After he graduated from high school, he went to Reed College. He didn't study there very long, but he stayed in the area. He liked to visit the college's calligraphy—artistic handwriting—classes. He learned a lot about design and used it years later with his products.

Jobs, Wozniak, and Ron Wayne started Apple Computer in 1976. In 1985, Apple fired him, so he started NeXT Computer, Inc. While he was working at NeXT, he met Laurene Powell, and they got married.

In 1996, Apple bought NeXT and Jobs once again worked at Apple. Under Jobs, Apple became very successful. In 2001, it introduced the iPod. In 2007, it sold the first iPhone. Three years later, the iPad came out.

Unfortunately, while Jobs was working at Apple, he got cancer. Medical treatments didn't cure him. In 2011, ten months after he turned 56, Steve Jobs died.

Part II. Complete the sentences with **before, after, when,** or **while.**

1. _____ Steve Jobs was attending high school, he worked for electronics businesses in the summer.

2. _____ he finished high school, he attended Reed College for a short time.

3. _____ he was living near Reed College, he visited calligraphy classes.

4. _____ he began NeXT Computer Inc., Apple fired him.

5. _____ Steve Jobs was working at Apple, the company introduced the iPod, iPhone, and iPad.

6. _____ Steve Jobs turned 57, he died.

Part III. Complete the sentences with the verbs you hear.

1. Steve Jobs _____ born in 1955.

2. While he _____ up in Palo Alto, California, he _____ interested in computers.

3. Jobs and Wozniak _____ their first computer together.

4. After Jobs _____ from high school, he _____ to Reed College.

5. He _____ there very long, but he _____ in the area.

6. He _____ a lot about calligraphy, and it _____ him with the design of his products.

7. In 1985, Apple _____ him, so he _____ NeXT Computer, Inc.

8. While he _____ at NeXT, he _____ Laurene Powell, and they got married.

9. Under Jobs, Apple _____ very successful.

10. Unfortunately, while Jobs _____ at Apple, he _____ cancer.

11. Medical treatments _____ cure him, and Jobs _____ in 2011.

❏ **Exercise 52. Looking at grammar.** (Chart 9-11)
Complete the sentences. Use the simple past or the past progressive form of the verbs in parentheses.

1. While my cousin and I (*have*) _____ dinner at a restaurant last night, we (*see*) _____ a friend of mine. I (*introduce*) _____ her to my cousin.

2. When I (*hear*) _____ a knock at the door last night, I (*walk*) _____ to the door and (*open*) _____ it. When I (*open*) _____ the door, I (*see*) _____ my brother. I (*greet*) _____ him and (*ask*) _____ him to come in.

3. When my cousin and I (*play*) _____ a video game last night, my brother (*call*) _____ me. He (*be*) _____ on the highway, and his car (*be*) _____ out of gas. I (*buy*) _____ gas and (*take*) _____ it to him.

4. While I (*walk*) _____ to class yesterday morning, I (*see*) _____ Abdullah. We (*say*) _____ hello.

❏ **Exercise 53. Looking at grammar.** (Chapter 9)
Choose the best completion.

1. I was surfing the Internet. I heard a knock on the door. When I heard the knock on the door, I _____ it.
   a. open
   b. am opening
   c. opened
   d. was opening

2. A: When _____ you talk to Jake?
   B: Yesterday.
   a. do
   b. are
   c. did
   d. were

3. I ____ TV when Gina called last night. We talked for an hour.
    a. watch   c. am watching
    b. watched   d. was watching

4. Mike is in his bedroom right now. He ____ , so we need to be quiet.
    a. is sleeping   c. slept
    b. sleeps   d. was sleeping

5. Kate ____ tell us the truth yesterday. She lied to us.
    a. don't   b. doesn't   c. didn't   d. wasn't

6. I saw a fish while I ____ in the ocean yesterday.
    a. swim   c. were swimming
    b. was swimming   d. swimming

7. When I heard the phone ring, I ____ it.
    a. answer   c. answered
    b. am answering   d. was answering

8. A: ____ you go to concerts often?
    B: Yes. I go at least once a month.
    a. Do   b. Did   c. Was   d. Were

9. While I ____ dinner last night, I burned my finger.
    a. cooking   b. cook   c. was cooking   d. was cook

10. Where ____ after work yesterday?
    a. you went   b. you did go   c. did you went   d. did you go

❑ **Exercise 54. Looking at grammar.** (Chapters 8 and 9)
Complete the sentences with the past form of the verbs in parentheses.

Part I.

    Yesterday (*be*) _____*was*_____ a terrible day. Everything (*go*) _____
                              1   2

wrong. First, I (*oversleep*) _____. My alarm clock (*ring, not*)
                                       3

_____. I (*wake*) _____ up when I (*hear*)
          4   5

_____ a noise outside my window. It was 9:15. I (*get*) _____
        6   7

dressed quickly. I (*run*) _____ to class, but I (*be*) _____ late.
                              8   9

The teacher (*be*) _____ upset with me.
                  10

Part II.

During a break, I (*go*) _____ outside. While I (*sit*)
                              11

_____ under a tree near the classroom building, I (*see*)
                12

_____ a friend. I (*call*) _____ to him. He (*join*)
        13   14

_____ me on the grass. We (*talk*) _____ about our
        15   16

classes. While we (*talk*) _____, I (*stand*) _____ up,
                                          17   18

(*step*) _____ in a hole, and (*break*) _____ my ankle.
                19   20

Part III.

My friend (*drive*) _____ me to the hospital. We (*go*) _____
                            21   22

to the emergency room. After the doctor (*take*) _____ X-rays of my ankle,
                                                          23

he (*put*) _____ a cast on it.
                  24

I (*pay*) _____ my bill. Then we (*leave*) _____
                  25   26

the hospital. My friend (*take*) _____ me home and (*help*)
                                          27

_____ me up the stairs to my apartment.
        28

Part IV.

When we (*get*) _____ to my apartment, I (*look*) _____
                        29   30

for my key in my purse and in my pockets. There was no key.

I (*ring*) _____ the doorbell. My roommate (*be, not*) _____
                 31   32

there, so I (*sit*) _____ down on the floor with my friend and (*wait*)
                        33

_____ for my roommate to get home.
         34

    Finally, my roommate (*come*) _____ home. I (*eat*) _____
                                               35   36

dinner quickly and (*go*) _____ to bed. While I (*sleep*) _____,
                                37   38

I (*dream*) _____ that I broke my arm. I hope my dream doesn't come true!
                  39

❏ **Exercise 55. Check your knowledge.** (Chapter 9)
Correct the mistakes.

              go
  1. Did you ~~went~~ downtown yesterday?

  2. Yesterday I speak to Ken before he leaves his office and goes home.

  3. I heared a good joke last night.

  4. When Pablo finished his work.

  5. I visitted my cousins in New York last month

  6. Where you did go yesterday afternoon?

  7. Ms. Wah was fly from Singapore to Tokyo last week.

  8. When I see my friend yesterday, he isn't speak to me.

  9. Why Mustafa didn't came to class last week?

10. Where you bought those shoes? I like them.

11. Mr. Adams teached our class last week.

12. Who you talk to?

13. Who did open the door? Jack openned it.

❏ **Exercise 56. Reading and writing.** (Chapter 9)

Part I. Read the paragraph. <u>Underline</u> the past verbs.

An Unforgettable Day

(1)   I remember February 28, 2001 very clearly. It <u>was</u> 12:00 in the afternoon, and

(2)   I was at home with my daughter. She was a year old, and we were having lunch.

(3)   There was a lot of noise outside our apartment building because builders were putting

(4)   on a new roof. Suddenly, I heard a very loud noise. The room began to move and

(5)   didn't stop. It was an earthquake! I grabbed my daughter and got under the kitchen

(6)   table. I told her everything was okay, but actually I felt afraid. The shaking lasted

(7)   about 45 seconds, but it felt longer. My husband was traveling that day, and I wanted

(8)   to talk to him. I tried to call him on his phone several times, but there was no cell

(9)   service. I was nervous, and I wasn't thinking very clearly. Finally, after ten minutes,

(10) I remembered the Internet. I checked and saw a news story about a very strong

(11) earthquake. Before I finished the article, my husband called. He was driving when

(12) he felt the earthquake, so he stopped at a gas station and waited. He was fine. Some

(13) buildings fell down in our city, but fortunately no one died.

Part II. Write about a day you remember well. Begin with this sentence: *I remember (date)* ***very clearly***.

Include this information in your paragraph:

1. What happened on that day?
2. When did it happen?
3. Where were you?
4. What were you doing?

5. Were other people there? What were they doing?
6. How did you feel?
7. How did the day/event end?

Part III. Editing check: Work individually or change papers with a partner. Check (✓) for the following:

1. _____ indented paragraph

2. _____ capital letter at the beginning of each sentence

3. _____ period at the end of each sentence

4. _____ correct use of past progressive for an activity in progress

5. _____ correct use of simple past for a completed activity

6. _____ correct spelling (use a dictionary or computer spell-check)

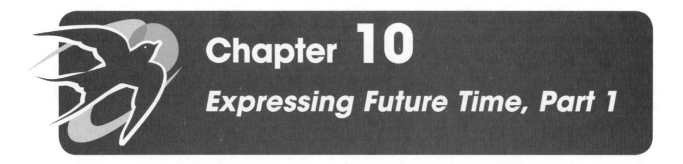

Chapter 10

Expressing Future Time, Part 1

❏ **Exercise 1. Warm-up.** (Chart 10-1)
Make the sentences true for you.

1. Yesterday I woke up at _____. Tomorrow I am going to wake up at _____.

2. Last night I ate dinner at _____. Tomorrow I am going to eat dinner at _____.

10-1 Future Time: Using *Be Going To*

(a) I **am going to go** downtown tomorrow. (b) Sue **is going to be** here tomorrow afternoon. (c) We **are going to come** to class tomorrow morning.	**Be going to** expresses (talks about) the future. FORM: **am** **is** } + **going to** + base form **are**	
(d) I**'m not going to go** downtown tomorrow. (e) Joe **isn't going to be** at the meeting tomorrow. (f) We **aren't going to eat** dinner early tonight.	NEGATIVE: **be** + **not** + **going to**	
(g) A: **Are** you **going to go** downtown tomorrow? 　　B: No, I'm not. (h) A: **Is** Jim **going to be** at the meeting tomorrow? 　　B: Yes, he is. (i) A: What time **are** we **going to eat** dinner tonight? 　　B: At eight.	QUESTION: **be** + *subject* + **going to** A form of **be** is used in the short answer to a yes/no question with **be going to**, as in (g) and (h). (See Chart 2-2, p. 30, for information about short answers with **be**.)	
(j) I'm **gonna** leave. (k) She's **gonna** stay.	In spoken English, *going to* is often pronounced "gonna." In formal written English, **going to** rather than *"gonna"* is used.	

❏ **Exercise 2. Looking at grammar.** (Chart 10-1)
Complete each sentence with the correct form of *be going to*.

Don't worry!

1. I am not late.   I   *am going to be*   on time.

2. We are not late.   We are going to be on time.

3. She is not late.   She is going to be on time.

4. You are not late.   You __are going to be__ on time.

5. They are not late.   They __are going to be__ on time.

6. Tim and I are not late.   Tim and I __are going to be__ on time.

7. Dr. Mason is not late.   Dr. Mason __is going to be__ on time.

8. Kyle and Sam are not late.   Kyle and Sam __are going to be__ on time.

❑ **Exercise 3. Let's talk: pairwork.** (Chart 10-1)
Part I. Work with a partner. Which of the given activities are you going to do tomorrow? Which ones are you not going to do tomorrow?

Example: go downtown
PARTNER A (*book open*):   Are you going to go downtown tomorrow?
PARTNER B (*book closed*):   Yes, I am. I'm going to go downtown tomorrow. OR
                  No, I'm not. I'm not going to go downtown tomorrow.

1. get up before eight o'clock
2. take a shower
3. make your bed
4. do the dishes
5. take a test
6. make a phone call
7. get a haircut
8. make dinner
9. make a mess in the kitchen
10. watch TV in the evening
11. go to bed early

Change roles.
12. get up early
13. get some exercise
14. walk to school
15. take a nap
16. do your laundry
17. do some ironing
18. go shopping
19. eat dinner alone
20. have dessert
21. chat with friends online
22. take a bath

Part II. Write three activities your partner is going to do tomorrow. Write three activities you are not going to do.

❏ **Exercise 4. Looking at grammar.** (Chart 10-1)
Complete the sentences. Use ***be going to*** and the words from the box (or your own words).

> ✓ call the manager   ✓ go to an Italian restaurant   ✓ take a sick day
> ✓ call the police   ✓ go to the park   ✓ take it to the post office
> ✓ get something to eat   lie down   ✓ take them to the laundromat
> ✓ go to the bookstore   ✓ take dance lessons   ✓ try to see the dentist today

1. I need to buy a textbook. I ___*am going to go to the bookstore.*___

2. Grace is hungry. She _is going to get something to eat._

3. My clothes are dirty. I _am going to take them to the laundromat._

4. I have a toothache. I _am going to try to see the dentist today._

5. George has to mail a package. He _is going to take it to the PO._

6. It's a nice day today. Molly and I _are going to go to the park._

7. Amanda and I want learn how to dance. We _are going to take dance lessons._

8. It's late at night. I hear a burglar! I _am going to call the police._

9. I feel terrible. I think I'm getting the flu. I _am going to take a sick day._

10. Ivan and Natasha want pizza. They _are going to go an Italian Restaurant._

11. Dana lives in an apartment. There's a problem with the plumbing. She _is going to call the manager._

Final Exam

Exercise 5. Let's talk: interview. (Chart 10-1)

Walk around the room. Ask and answer questions using **be going to**. Write down your classmates' names and their answers. Share some of their answers with the class.

Example: when \ go downtown
STUDENT A: When are you going to go downtown?
STUDENT B: Tomorrow afternoon. / In a couple of days. / Around noon. / Etc.

QUESTION	FIRST NAME	ANSWER
1. where \ go after class today	Mr. Messi	going to the mosque
2. what time \ get home tonight	Nawaf	at 8 pm.
3. when \ eat dinner	Yugi	maybe 5 pm
4. where \ eat dinner	Khalifa	at MV
5. what time \ go to bed tonight	Ken	at 8 pm.
6. what time \ get up tomorrow morning	Aziz	at 3am
7. where \ be tomorrow morning		
8. when \ finish your English studies		
9. where \ live next year		
10. when \ take a trip and where \ go		

☐ Exercise 6. Game. (Chart 10-1)

Work in teams. Your teacher will ask you a question. Discuss the answer. Raise your hand when you are ready. The first team to give a correct answer gets a point. Close your book for this activity.

Example: You want to buy some tea. What are you going to do?
TEAM A STUDENT: I'm going to go to the grocery store.

1. You have a toothache.
   What are you going to do?
2. You need to mail a package.
   Where are you going to go?
3. Your clothes are dirty.
4. It's midnight. You're sleepy.
5. It's late at night. You hear a burglar.
6. You need to buy some groceries.
7. You want to go swimming.
8. You want to go fishing.
9. You want to buy a new coat.
10. You're hungry.
11. You have a headache.
12. It's a nice day today.
13. You need to cash a check.
14. You want some (pizza) for dinner.
15. You're reading a book. You don't know the meaning of a word.

□ **Exercise 7. Warm-up.** (Chart 10-2)
Check <u>all</u> (✓) the sentences that have a future meaning.

1. ____ I am flying to Montreal tomorrow.

2. ____ My aunt and uncle are meeting me at the airport.

3. ____ They are going to have their 50th anniversary next week.

10-2 Using the Present Progressive to Express Future Time

(a) Sue	*is going to leave*	at 8:00 tomorrow.	Sometimes the present progressive is used to express future time.
(b) Sue	*is leaving*	at 8:00 tomorrow.	Examples (a) and (b) mean the same thing.
(c) We	*are going to drive*	to Toronto next week.	Examples (c) and (d) mean the same thing.
(d) We	*are driving*	to Toronto next week.	The present progressive is used for future meaning when the speaker is talking about plans that have already been made.

COMMON VERBS

come	drive	go	meet	spend	stay
do	fly	leave	return	start	take

□ **Exercise 8. Looking at grammar.** (Chart 10-2)
Rewrite the sentences using the present progressive.

A trip to Greece

1. My mother and I are going to leave for our trip at 10:00 tomorrow.

   My mother and I are leaving for our trip at 10:00 tomorrow.

2. We are going to fly to Athens. We are flying to Athens.

3. We are going to spend a week there. We are spending a week there.

4. My father is going to meet us there. We are meeting us there.

5. He is going to take the train. He is taking the train.

6. We are going to go sightseeing together. We are

7. I am going to come back by boat, and they are going to return by train.
   I am coming back by boat and they are returning by train.

Expressing Future Time, Part 1 **307**

Exercise 9. Listening. (Chart 10-2)

Listen to each sentence. Decide if the meaning is present or future time.

Example: You will hear: We are meeting later this afternoon.
You will choose: present   (future)

1. present	future	5. present	future
2. present	future	6. present	future
3. present	future	7. present	future
4. present	future	8. present	future

Exercise 10. Let's talk: interview. (Chart 10-2)

Walk around the room. Ask and answer questions using the present progressive. Write down your classmates' names and answers. Share some of their answers with the class.

Example: what \ do \ tonight
STUDENT A: What are you doing tonight?
STUDENT B: I'm staying home and watching a DVD.

QUESTION	FIRST NAME	ANSWER
1. where \ go \ after school		
2. what time \ have dinner		
3. when \ go \ to bed tonight		
4. what time \ get up \ tomorrow		
5. what \ do \ tomorrow		
6. what \ do \ this weekend		

Exercise 11. Listening. (Charts 10-1 and 10-2)

Listen to each sentence. Choose the verb you hear.

Example: You will hear: It's going to rain tomorrow.
You will choose: (a.) is going to rain   b. is raining   c. rains

1. a. am going to leave   b. am leaving   c. leave
2. a. is going to start   b. is starting   c. starts
3. (a.) is going to come   b. is coming   c. comes
4. a. is going to call   b. is calling   c. calls
5. a. Are you going to study   b. Are you studying   c. Do you study
6. a. are going to have   (b.) are having   c. have
7. a. aren't going to go   b. aren't going   c. don't go
8. a. is going to eat   b. is eating   c. eats
9. a. is going to help   b. is helping   c. helps

❏ **Exercise 12. Let's talk: small groups.** (Charts 10-1 and 10-2)
Your group won a contest and received a lot of money. (As a class, decide on the amount.) You can use it for one of the four situations. What are you going to do with the money? Choose one situation and talk about your plans.

1. The money is to help other people. What are you going to do?
2. The money is to improve your school. What are you going to do?
3. The money is to make the world a better place. What are you going to do?
4. The money is for a wonderful vacation for your class. Where are you going to go and what are you going to do?

❏ **Exercise 13. Warm-up.** (Chart 10-3)
Choose the correct completion.

1. I studied English   last week / next week.
2. I am going to take a break   a few minutes ago / in a few minutes.
3. I did homework   last night / tomorrow night.

10-3 Words Used for Past Time and Future Time

PAST	FUTURE	
yesterday	tomorrow	PAST: It *rained* **yesterday**. FUTURE: It*'s going to rain* **tomorrow**.
yesterday morning yesterday afternoon yesterday evening last night	tomorrow morning tomorrow afternoon tomorrow evening tomorrow night	PAST: I *was* in class **yesterday morning**. FUTURE: I*'m going to be* in class **tomorrow morning**.
last week last month last year last weekend last spring last summer last fall last winter last Monday, etc.	next week next month next year next weekend next spring next summer next fall next winter next Monday, etc.	PAST: Mary *went* downtown **last week**. FUTURE: Mary *is going to go* downtown **next week**. PAST: Bob *graduated* from high school **last spring**. FUTURE: Ann *is going to graduate* from high school **next spring**.
. . . minutes ago . . . hours ago . . . days ago . . . weeks ago . . . months ago . . . years ago	in . . . minutes (from now) in . . . hours (from now) in . . . days (from now) in . . . weeks (from now) in . . . months (from now) in . . . years (from now)	PAST: I *finished* my homework **five minutes ago**. FUTURE: Pablo *is going to finish* his homework **in five minutes**.

❏ **Exercise 14. Looking at grammar.** (Chart 10-3)

Complete the sentences. Use *yesterday*, *last*, *tomorrow*, or *next*.

1. I went swimming ___*yesterday*___ morning.

2. Alberto is going to go to the beach ___*tomorrow*___ morning.

3. I'm going to take a trip ___next___ week.

4. Diana went to Miami ___last___ week for a short vacation.

5. We had a test in class ___yesterday___ afternoon.

6. ___Tomorrow___ afternoon we're going to look for a used car.

7. My friend bought a used car ___last___ Friday.

8. My sister is going to arrive ___next___ Tuesday.

9. My brother is going to enter the university ___next___ fall.

10. ___Last___ spring I took a trip to San Francisco.

11. Mia is going to fly to London ___next___ month.

12. Zack lived in Tokyo ___last___ year.

13. I'm going to study at the library ___last___ night.

14. ___Yesterday___ night I watched TV.

15. ___Tomorrow___ evening I'm going to go to a baseball game.

16. Mrs. Chang went to a basketball game ___yesterday___ evening.

☐ **Exercise 15. Grammar and speaking.** (Chart 10-3)

Part I. Complete the questions with time expressions.

1. What did you do _____?

2. What are you going to do _____?

3. Where are you going to be in _winter_____?

4. Where were you _this morning - this evening_

5. Where did you go last _____?

6. Where are you going to go next _____?

7. What are you going to do tomorrow _____?

8. What did you do yesterday _____?

Part II. Work with a partner. Ask and answer questions. Share a few of your partner's answers with the class.

☐ **Exercise 16. Looking at grammar.** (Chart 10-3)

Complete the sentences. Use the given time expressions with *ago* or *in*.

1. ten minutes   Class is going to end ___in ten minutes._____

2. ten minutes   Hanan's class ended ___ten minutes ago._____

3. an hour   The post office isn't open. It closed _an hour ago___

4. an hour   Yoshi is going to call us _in an hour.___

5. two months   I'm studying abroad now, but I'm going to be back home _in two months.___

6. two months   My wife and I took a trip to Morocco _two months ago.___

7. a minute   Karen left _a minute ago.___

8. half an hour   I'm going to meet Peter at the coffee shop _in half an hour___

9. one week   The new highway is going to open _in one week___

10. a year   I was living in Korea _a year ago.___

❑ **Exercise 17. Let's talk: pairwork.** (Chart 10-3)

Work with a partner. Change the sentences using **ago** or **in**. Use the calendar to calculate length of time. "Today" is September 9th.

1. Brad is going to leave his old job as a hotel chef on September 12th.

   → *Brad is going leave his old job in three days.*

2. He is going to start a new job as a chef at a famous restaurant on September 14th.

3. Brad graduated from cooking school in Paris on June 9th.

4. He is going to be in a cooking competition on September 23rd.

5. Brad began taking cooking classes in 2009.

6. He moved to Paris a year later.

7. Brad is going to cook for a TV show on Septem

8. Brad is going to marry his high school sweethea

SEPTEMBER						
Sun.	Mon.	Tues.	Wed.	Thurs.	Fri.	Sat.
1	2	3	4	5	6	7
8	9	10	11	12	13	14

Handwritten notes:
1- He is Starting a new Job in 5 days
2- brad graduated from cooking school 3 months ago
3- in 14 days
4- 13 Years ago

❑ **Exercise 18. Listening.** (Chart 10-3)

Listen to the beginning of each sentence. Choose th

Example: You will hear: Rudi is going to finish h

You will choose: a. five minutes ago.   ⓑ in five minutes.

1. a. one hour ago.   ⓑ in one hour.

2. ⓐ two weeks ago.   b. in two weeks.

3. ⓐ one year ago.   b. in one year.

4. a. ten minutes ago.   ⓑ in ten minutes.

5. ⓐ a few minutes ago.   b. in a few minutes.

6. ⓐ last spring.   b. next spring.

7. a. last summer.   ⓑ next summer.

8. a. last weekend.   ⓑ next weekend.

9. ⓐ yesterday evening.   b. tomorrow evening.

❑ **Exercise 19. Let's talk: interview.** (Chart 10-3)

Walk around the room. Ask a different student each pair of questions. Write down the names of the students and their answers. Share some of their answers with the class.

Example: what \ do \ yesterday?
STUDENT A: What did you do yesterday?
STUDENT B: I stayed home and studied for a test.

Example: what \ do \ tomorrow?

STUDENT A: What are you going to do tomorrow?

STUDENT B: I'm going to go to a party with my friends.

QUESTION	FIRST NAME	ANSWERS
1. where \ go \ yesterday? *Where did you go yesterday?* *Where are you going tomorrow?* where \ go \ tomorrow?	Lihua	
2. who \ call \ last week? *Who did you call last week?* *Who are you calling next week?* who \ call \ next week?	Aziz	
3. who \ call \ yesterday? *Who did you call yesterday?* who \ call \ tomorrow?	Matar	
4. what \ watch on TV \ last week? what \ watch on TV \ next week?		
5. where \ live \ five years ago? where \ live \ in five years?		

❏ **Exercise 20. Looking at grammar.** (Chart 10-3)

Complete the sentences. Use *yesterday*, *last*, *tomorrow*, *next*, *in*, or *ago*.

1. I went to the zoo _____*last*_____ week.

2. Yolanda Matos went to the zoo a week _____.

3. Charles Nelson is going to go to the park _____ Saturday.

4. We're going to go to the park _____ two days.

5. My kids went to the pool _____ morning.

6. My cousin is going to go to the circus _____ afternoon.

7. Kim Yang-Don graduated from Sogang University _____ spring.

8. We're going to have company for dinner _____ night.

9. We had company for dinner three days _____.

10. We're going to have dinner at our friends' house _____ two days.

11. _____ evening we're going to go to a concert.

12. _____ Friday I went to a party.

13. _____ afternoon the students took a test.

14. My stepsister arrived here _____ month.

15. She is going to leave _____ two weeks.

16. _____ year Kyoko is going to be a freshman in college.

❏ **Exercise 21. Warm-up.** (Chart 10-4)
Read the sentences and choose the correct number.

1. Dave left a couple of weeks ago.   two   five

2. JoAnn is going to get married in a few months.   one   four

10-4 Using *A Couple Of* or *A Few* with *Ago* (Past) and *In* (Future)

(a) Sam arrived here **one** (OR **a**) *year ago*. (b) Jack is going to be here *in **two** minutes*. (c) I talked to Ann ***three*** *days ago*.	Numbers are often used in time expressions with **ago** and **in**.
(d) I saw Carlos *a **couple of** months ago*. (e) He's going to return to Mexico *in a **couple of** months*. (f) I got a letter from Gina *a **few** weeks ago*. (g) I'm going to see Gina *in a **few** weeks*.	***A couple of*** and ***a few*** are also commonly used. ***A couple of*** means "two." *A couple of months ago = two months ago* ***A few*** means "a small number, not a large number." *A few weeks ago = two, three, four, or five weeks ago*
(h) I began college last year. I'm going to graduate *in **two more** years*. My sister is almost finished with her education. She's going to graduate *in a **few more** months*.	Frequently, the word ***more*** is used in future time expressions that begin with **in**.

Read the paragraph. Then, as a class, decide if the statements are true or false.

Love at First Sight?

   Ben and Jen met September 15, 2009. It was the first day of college for them. They were in chemistry class. Ben fell in love with Jen a few days later. Ben asked Jen to marry him on January 1. Jen gave him her answer a couple of days later. She wasn't sure, so she said "no." A couple of months later, she changed her mind. They got married a few months after that. A couple of years later they had their first child. They are very happy together.

1. Ben fell in love with Jen on September 16.	T	F
2. Jen told Ben "no" in January.	T	F
3. Jen changed her mind in March.	T	F
4. Ben and Jen got married in April.	T	F
5. They had their first child in 2013.	T	F

❑ **Exercise 23. Let's talk: small groups.** (Chart 10-4)
Work in small groups. Take turns completing the sentences. Use information from your own life. Use the given words with **ago** or **in**. Use numbers (*one, two, three, ten, sixteen, etc.*) or the expressions **a couple of** or **a few**.

1. days   We studied Chapter 9 _____ *a couple of days ago / three days ago / etc.* _____

2. days   We're going to finish this chapter _____ *in a few more days / in three or* _____
                       four days / etc. _____

3. hours   I ate breakfast _____

4. hours   I'm going to eat lunch/dinner _____

5. minutes   We finished Exercise 22 _____

6. minutes   This class is going to end _____

7. years   I was born _____

8. years   My parents got married _____

9. weeks ⎫   I arrived in this city _____, and I'm going
    months ⎬
    years   ⎭   to leave this city _____

□ Exercise 24. Looking at grammar. (Chart 10-4)

Complete the sentences with your own words. Write about your life. For example, what did you do a few days ago? What are you going to do in a few days? Share some of your sentences with the class.

1. _____ a few days ago.

2. _____ in a few days.

3. _____ in a few more minutes.

4. _____ three hours ago.

5. _____ in four more hours.

6. _____ a couple of days ago.

7. _____ in a couple of months.

8. _____ many years ago.

9. _____ in a couple of minutes.

□ Exercise 25. Listening. (Chart 10-4)

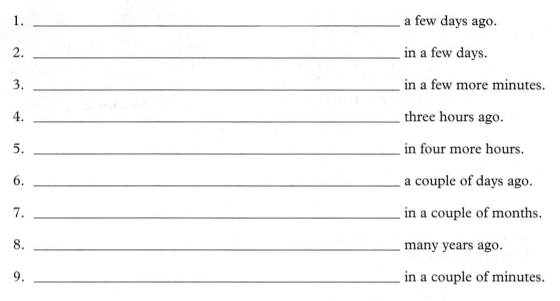

Listen to the sentences. Choose *same* if the sentence below has the same meaning. Choose *different* if the meaning is different.

Example: You will hear: Liam graduated from high school a few years ago.
You will read: Liam graduated from high school two years ago.
You will choose: (same)   different

1. Jean is going to leave in two days.	same	different
2. Lena is going to leave in three weeks.	same	different
3. We sold our house five years ago.	same	different
4. The phone rang five minutes ago.	same	different
5. Marc is going to be here in fifteen minutes.	same	different

□ Exercise 26. Warm-up. (Chart 10-5)

Underline the time phrase in each sentence. Check (✓) the sentence that has a present meaning.

1. _____ I am working this morning.

2. _____ I worked this morning.

3. _____ I am going to work this morning.

10-5 Using *Today, Tonight,* and *This* + *Morning, Afternoon, Evening, Week, Month, Year*

PRESENT	Right now it's 10:00 A.M. We are in our English class. (a) We **are studying** English **this morning**.	today tonight this morning this afternoon this evening this week this weekend this month this year	These words can express present, past, or future time.
PAST	Right now it's 10:00 A.M. Nancy left home at 9:00 to go downtown. She isn't at home right now. (b) Nancy **went** downtown **this morning**.		
FUTURE	Right now it's 10:00 A.M. Class ends at 11:00. After class today, I'm going to go to the bank. (c) I**'m going to go** to the bank **this morning**.		

❏ **Exercise 27. Looking at grammar.** (Chart 10-5)
Answer the questions orally or in writing (on a separate piece of paper).

1. What did you do earlier this year? → *I came to this city earlier this year.*
2. What are you doing this year?
3. What are you going to do this year?
4. What did you do earlier today?
5. What are you doing today, right now?
6. What are you going to do later today?
7. What did you do earlier this morning / afternoon / evening?
8. What are you going to do later this morning / afternoon / evening?

❏ **Exercise 28. Looking at grammar.** (Chart 10-5)
Choose all the correct time expressions.

1. What are you doing _____?
   a. this morning
   b. this week
   c. tonight
   d. this afternoon
   e. today

2. What did you do _____?
   a. this week
   b. this month
   c. today
   d. this year
   e. this evening

3. What are you going to do _____?
   a. this morning
   b. this weekend
   c. tonight
   d. this year
   e. today

❑ **Exercise 29. Let's talk: small groups.** (Chart 10-5)

Work in small groups. Take turns being Student A and asking your classmates questions about future activities. Student A will ask two questions with ***When***.

Example: go downtown
STUDENT A: When are you going to go downtown?
STUDENT B: This weekend. / Tomorrow morning. / In a couple of days. / Etc.
STUDENT A: When is (*Student B*) going to go downtown?
STUDENT C: He/She is going to go downtown this weekend.

1. have dinner
2. do your grammar homework
3. go shopping
4. go to (*name of a class*)
5. visit (*name of a place in this city*)
6. call (*name of a student*) on the phone

7. go to (*name of a restaurant*) for dinner
8. see your family again
9. buy a car
10. see (*name of a new movie*)
11. go to (*name of an event*)
12. take a vacation

❑ **Exercise 30. Let's talk: pairwork.** (Chart 10-5)

Work with a partner. Ask questions using the verbs from the box or your own words.

Example: tomorrow morning
PARTNER A: Are you going to come to class tomorrow morning?
PARTNER B: Yes, I am. OR No, I'm not.

Example: yesterday morning
PARTNER A: Did you eat breakfast yesterday morning?
PARTNER B: Yes, I did. OR No, I didn't.

buy	do	eat	send	visit
call	drink	get up	shop	wake up
come	drive	go	sleep	wash

1. last night
2. tomorrow night
3. tonight
4. tomorrow afternoon
5. yesterday afternoon
6. this afternoon
7. last Friday
8. next Friday
9. next week

Change roles.
10. last week
11. this week
12. yesterday morning
13. tomorrow morning
14. this morning
15. later today
16. a couple of hours ago
17. in a couple of hours
18. this evening

❑ **Exercise 31. Listening.** (Chart 10-5)

Listen to each sentence. Decide if the meaning is past, present, or future time.

Example: You will hear: The students are busy working on a project in the classroom.

You will choose: past (present) future

1. past	present	future		6. past	present	future
2. past	present	future		7. past	present	future
3. past	present	future		8. past	present	future
4. past	present	future		9. past	present	future
5. past	present	future		10. past	present	future

❑ **Exercise 32. Warm-up.** (Chart 10-6)

Check (✓) the sentences with a future meaning.

1. ____ The test is going to be long.   3. ____ The test was long.

2. ____ The test is long.   4. ____ The test will be long.

10-6 Future Time: Using *Will*

AFFIRMATIVE STATEMENT	(a) Mike **will arrive** at 10:00 tomorrow. (b) Mike **is going to arrive** at 10:00 tomorrow.	Examples (a) and (b) have basically the same meaning.

	(c) CORRECT: Mike **will go** there.
	  INCORRECT: *Mike will goes there.*
	  INCORRECT: *Mike wills go there.*
		The base form of a verb follows **will**. In (c): *goes* and *wills go* are NOT correct.

	(d) CORRECT: Mike **will arrive** at 10:00. INCORRECT: *Mike will arrives at 10:00.*	There is never a final **-s** on **will** for future time.
	(e) CORRECT: Mike **will go** there. INCORRECT: *Mike will to go there.*	**Will** is not followed by an infinitive with **to**. In (e): *will to go* is not correct.
CONTRACTIONS	(f) I will come. = **I'll** come. You will come. = **You'll** come. She will come. = **She'll** come. He will come. = **He'll** come. It will come. = **It'll** come. We will come. = **We'll** come. They will come. = **They'll** come.	**Will** is contracted to **'ll** with subject pronouns.* These contractions are common in both speaking and writing.
NEGATIVE STATEMENT	(g) Bob **will not be** here tomorrow. (h) Bob **won't be** here tomorrow.	NEGATIVE CONTRACTION **will** + **not** = **won't**

*__Will__ is also often contracted with nouns in speaking (but not in writing).

  WRITTEN: *Tom will be here at ten.*
  SPOKEN: *"Tom'll be here at ten."*

❑ **Exercise 33. Let's talk: class activity.** (Chart 10-6)
Change the sentences by using **will** to express future time.

1. Mrs. Ortega is going to need some help tomorrow.

  → Mrs. Ortega will need some help tomorrow.

2. Lev and Olga are going to help her.

3. The train is going to be late. *the train will be late*

4. Hurry up, or we're going to miss the beginning of the concert.

5. I'm not going to be at home this evening. *want*

6. Kelly is going to wait for us at the bus stop. *will not be*

7. Be careful with those scissors! You're going to hurt yourself!

8. You are going to have two science classes next term, not one.

❑ **Exercise 34. Let's talk: small groups.** (Chart 10-6)
Work in small groups. What is going to happen in the lives of your classmates in the next 50 years? Make predictions about your classmates' futures. Share some of your predictions with the class.

Example:
STUDENT A: Greta is going to become a famous research scientist.
STUDENT B: Ali will have a happy marriage and lots of children.
STUDENT C: Armando will live in a quiet place and write books.★
       Etc.

❑ **Exercise 35. Listening.** (Chart 10-6)
Part I. Listen to each pair of sentences and note the contractions with **will**.

1. a. The doctor will see you in a few minutes. OR
   b. The doctor'll see you in a few minutes.

2. a. Mom will be home late. OR
   b. Mom'll be home late.

3. a. Bob will pick us up. OR
   b. Bob'll pick us up.

Part II. Complete the sentences with the words you hear: **will** or **'ll**.

1. The nurse _____*ll*_____ give you some medicine.

2. Your headache _____ go away quickly.

3. The weather ____*will*____ be nice tomorrow.

4. Sorry, dinner ____*will*____ be late tonight.

★When two verbs are connected by *and,* the helping verbs **be going to** and **will** are usually not repeated.
 For example: *I'm going to lock the doors and ~~am going to~~ turn out the lights.*
        I'll lock the doors and ~~will~~ turn out the lights.

5. The bus _Will_ be here in a few minutes.

6. Dad _____ help you with your homework later.

7. The students _wi11_ need more time for review.

❏ **Exercise 36. Warm-up.** (Chart 10-7)
Answer the questions.

1. Will you be here next year?   Yes, I will.   No, I won't.
2. Will you be a student next year?   Yes, I will.   No, I won't.
3. Will you graduate next year?   Yes, I will.   No, I won't.

10-7 Asking Questions with *Will*

QUESTION					ANSWER
(QUESTION WORD) +	*WILL* +	SUBJECT +	MAIN VERB		
(a)	*Will*	*Tom*	*come*	tomorrow? →	*Yes, he will.* *No, he won't.*
(b)	*Will*	*you*	*be*	at home tonight? →	*Yes, I will.* *No, I won't.*
(c) When	*will*	*Ann*	*arrive?*	→	*Next Saturday.*
(d) What time	*will*	*the plane*	*arrive?*	→	*Three-thirty.*
(e) Where	*will*	*you*	*be*	tonight? →	*At home.*

*NOTE: **Will** is not contracted with a pronoun in a short answer. See Chart 2-2, p. 30, for information about the use of contractions in short answers.

❏ **Exercise 37. Looking at grammar.** (Chart 10-7)
Make questions.

1. A: _____Will you be at home tomorrow night?_____

   B: Yes, _____I will._____ (I'll be at home tomorrow night.)

2. A: _____Will Mona be in class tomorrow?_____

   B: No, _____she won't._____ (Mona won't be in class tomorrow).

3. A: _____When will you see Mr. Lu?_____

   B: Tomorrow afternoon. (I'll see Mr. Lu tomorrow afternoon.)

4. A: _Will the plane arrive on time?_

   B: Yes, _It will_ (The plane will be on time.)

5. A: ~~When~~ Will dinner be ready in a few minutes?

B: Yes, It will _____ (Dinner will be ready in a few minutes.)

6. A: When will dinner be ready?

B: In a few minutes. (Dinner will be ready in a few minutes.)

7. A: When will you graduate?

B: Next year. (I'll graduate next year.)

8. A: Where will Elyse go to school next year?

B: At the community college. (Elyse will go to school at the community college next year.)

9. A: Will Jenna and Scott be at the party?

B: No, they won't _____ (Jenna and Scott won't be at the party.)

10. A: Will Martin arrive in Chicago next week?

B: Yes, He will _____ (Martin will arrive in Chicago next week.)

11. A: Where will Martin in next week?

B: In Chicago. (Martin will be in Chicago next week.)

12. A: Will you be home early tonigh?

B: No, I won't _____ (I won't be home early tonight.)

13. A: Will Dr. Fernandez be back?

B: In a few minutes. (Dr. Fernandez will be back in a few minutes.)

14. A: Will we be ready to leave at 8:15?

B: Yes, we will _____ (We'll be ready to leave at 8:15.)

❑ **Exercise 38. Let's talk: pairwork.** (Chart 10-7)

Part I. Imagine you are visiting Paris. Check (✓) the fun things you will do on your trip.

Paris activities:

____ visit the Eiffel Tower

____ ride the elevator to the top

____ drink coffee in a French café

____ buy a painting from a street artist

____ ride a boat on the Seine River

_____ see the *Mona Lisa* at the Louvre museum

_____ speak French

_____ buy some clothes at a designer shop

_____ eat dinner in an expensive French restaurant

_____ visit Notre Dame cathedral

_____ take a bus tour of Paris

_____ buy some French perfume

Part II. Work with a partner. Take turns asking and answering questions about your activities.

Example: visit the Eiffel Tower
PARTNER A: Will you visit the Eiffel Tower?
PARTNER B: Yes, I will. OR No, I won't.
PARTNER A: Your turn now.

PARTNER A	PARTNER B
1. visit the Eiffel Tower	1. ride the elevator to the top
2. drink coffee in a French café	2. buy a painting from a street artist
3. ride a boat on the Seine River	3. see the *Mona Lisa* at the Louvre museum
4. speak French	4. buy some clothes at a designer shop
5. eat dinner in an expensive French restaurant	5. visit Notre Dame cathedral
6. take a bus tour of Paris	6. buy some French perfume

❑ **Exercise 39. Listening.** (Chart 10-7)

You are going away on a dream vacation. Where would you like to visit? It can be a small town, a big city, a country, or a place far away from cities or towns. Write it down. Then listen to each question and write a short answer. Share a few of your answers.

Place: _____

1. _I will go n_____

2. _____

3. _____

4. _____

5. _What you will doo there_____

Exercise 40. Reading, listening, and speaking. (Chart 10-7)
Part I. Read the story. Then listen to the questions and choose the correct answers.

SITUATION: Samantha is a high school student. She is thinking about next year. New Year's is in one week. She wants to change some of her habits. She is making some New Year's resolutions.

Samantha's New Year's Resolutions

    Samantha is a good student. She studies a lot, but she likes to go to parties on weekends. She wants to attend a good university, so next year she will study on weekends too. She has a healthy lifestyle, but sometimes she forgets to exercise. She will exercise four times a week. Now, she exercises only two times a week. She doesn't smoke, but she wants to lose a little weight. She will start a new diet next year. Samantha loves her grandmother, but she doesn't see her very much. Samantha misses her. Next year, she will visit her grandmother once a week. Samantha is planning a lot of changes, and she thinks she will be happier.

1. (Yes, she will.)   No, she won't.

2. Yes, she will.   No, she won't.

3. Yes, she will.   No, she won't.

4. Yes, she will.   No, she won't.

5. Yes, she will.   No, she won't.

6. Yes, she will.   No, she won't.

7. Yes, she will.   No, she won't.

8. Yes, she will.   No, she won't.

Part II. Imagine it is New Year's and you are making some resolutions. What are some things you are going to do/will do to improve yourself and your life this year? Make a list. Then share some of your ideas with the class.

Example: I will stop smoking.
          I am going to get more exercise.
          Etc.

❏ **Exercise 41. Listening.** (Chart 10-7)
Won't and *want* sound similar. Listen carefully to the sentences and choose the verbs you hear.

1. won't   (want)

2. won't   want

3. won't   want

4. won't   want

5. won't   want

6. won't   want

7. won't   want

8. won't   want

10-8 Verb Summary: Present, Past, and Future

	STATEMENT: AFFIRMATIVE	STATEMENT: NEGATIVE	QUESTION
SIMPLE PRESENT	I *eat* lunch every day. She *eats* lunch every day.	I *don't eat* lunch. She *doesn't eat* lunch.	*Do* you *eat* lunch? *Does* she *eat* lunch?
PRESENT PROGRESSIVE	I *am eating* lunch right now. She *is eating* lunch. They *are eating* lunch.	I*'m not eating* lunch. She *isn't eating* lunch. They *aren't eating* lunch.	*Am* I *eating* lunch? *Is* she *eating* lunch? *Are* they *eating* lunch?
SIMPLE PAST	He *ate* lunch yesterday.	He *didn't eat* lunch.	*Did* he *eat* lunch?
BE GOING TO	I *am going to eat* lunch tomorrow. She *is going to eat* lunch tomorrow. They *are going to eat* lunch tomorrow.	I*'m not going to eat* lunch tomorrow. She *isn't going to eat* lunch tomorrow. They *aren't going to eat* lunch tomorrow.	*Am* I *going to eat* lunch tomorrow? *Is* she *going to eat* lunch tomorrow? *Are* they *going to eat* lunch tomorrow?
WILL	He *will eat* lunch tomorrow.	He *won't eat* lunch tomorrow.	*Will* he *eat* lunch tomorrow?

❑ **Exercise 42. Looking at grammar.** (Chart 10-8)
Complete the sentences with the verbs in parentheses.

1. Right now Marta (*sit*) _____is sitting_____

   at her desk.

2. She (*do, not*) __didn't do her homework__

   homework. She (*chat*) _chatting chatted_

   online with her parents.

3. She (*chat*) __will chat chats__ with

   them every week.

4. She (*chat, not*) __doesn't chat__

   with them every day.

5. Her parents (*expect, not*) __don't expect__ to talk to her every day.

6. Last night Marta (*send*) _____Sent_____ an email to her brother. Then she

   (*start*) _____ to text her sister.

7. While Marta was texting her sister, her phone (*ring*) _____rang_____ . It was her

   best friend.

8. Marta (*finish, not*) _____doesn't finish_____ the text. After she (*talk*)

   _____ to her friend, she (*go*) _____ to bed.

9. Tomorrow she (*call*) _____will call_____ her sister.

10. Marta (*chat, not*) _____isn't chatting_____ with her parents tomorrow.

11. (*you, chat*) _____Do you chat_____ online with someone every day?

12. (*you, chat*) _____Did you chat_____ online with someone yesterday?

13. (*you, chat*) _____Will you chat_____ online with someone tomorrow?

❑ **Exercise 43. Listening.** (Chart 10-8)

Listen to the sentences. Write the verbs you hear.

A restaurant meal

1. Bert _____ meat, eggs, or fish.

2. He's a vegetarian. He _____ meat. He _____

   _____ it as a child either.

3. His wife, Beth, _____ meat, but she isn't a vegetarian.

4. She _____ the taste of meat.

5. They _____ a new restaurant tomorrow.

6. It _____ last month, and online reviews _____ it is

   excellent.

7. Bert _____ probably _____ a dish with lots of vegetables.

8. Beth _____ vegetables for a main dish. She _____

   probably _____ for some type of fish.

9. _____ themselves?

10. _____ back to this restaurant?

10-9 Verb Summary: Forms of *Be*

	STATEMENT: AFFIRMATIVE	STATEMENT: NEGATIVE	QUESTION
SIMPLE PRESENT	I *am* from South Korea. He *is* from Egypt. They *are* from Venezuela.	I *am not* from Jordan. She *isn't* from Egypt. They *aren't* from Italy.	*Am* I from Chile? *Is* she from Greece? *Are* they from Kenya?
SIMPLE PAST	Ann *was* late yesterday. They *were* late yesterday.	She *wasn't* on time. They *weren't* on time.	*Was* she late? *Were* they late?
BE GOING TO	I *am going to be* on time. She *is going to be* on time. They *are going to be* on time.	I'*m not going to be* late. She *isn't going to be* late. They *aren't going to be* late.	*Am* I *going to be* on time? *Is* she *going to be* on time? *Are* they *going to be* on time?
WILL	He *will be* absent.	He *won't be* in class.	*Will* he *be* absent?

❏ **Exercise 44. Looking at grammar.** (Chart 10-9)
Complete the sentences with the verbs in parentheses.

1. I (*be*) ___am___ in class right now. I (*be, not*) ___wasn't___ here yesterday.
   I (*be*) ___was___ absent yesterday. (*you, be*) ___Were you___ in class
   yesterday? (*Carmen, be*) ___Was Carmen___ here yesterday?

2. Carmen and I (*be*) ___were___ absent from class yesterday. We (*be, not*)
   ___weren't___ here.

3. My friends (*be*) ___are going to be___ at Fatima's apartment tomorrow evening. I (*be*)
   ___am going to be___ there too. (*you, be*) ___are you going to be___ there? (*Akira, be*)
   ___are Akira going to be___ there?

4. A whale (*be, not*) ___isn't___ a fish. It (*be*) _____ a mammal.
   Dolphins (*be, not*) _____ fish either. They (*be*) _____ mammals.

a dolphin

a whale

❑ **Exercise 45. Looking at grammar.** (Charts 10-8 and 10-9)
Complete the questions with *Are* or *Do*.

SITUATION: Rebecca's daughter is starting fourth grade this morning. Her mother is asking her questions.

1. _____*Do*_____ you want to get there early?

2. _____*Are*_____ you excited?

3. _____ you have your notebook?

4. _____ you remember your teacher's name?

5. _____ you a little scared?

6. _____ you have your lunch money?

7. _____ you ready to go?

8. _____ you okay?

9. _____ you want me to be quiet?

❑ **Exercise 46. Looking at grammar.** (Charts 10-8 and 10-9)
Complete the sentences with *Were* or *Did*.

SITUATION: Jeff has a hard job and works long hours. He got home at 3:00 A.M. Now it's later in the morning, and his roommates are asking him questions.

1. _____ you at your office?

2. _____ you stay late?

3. _____ you have a lot of work?

4. _____ you busy?

5. _____ you tired when you got home?

6. _____ you feel tired?

7. _____ you drink a lot of coffee?

8. _____ you hungry at 3:00 A.M.?

9. _____ you go to bed late?

❑ **Exercise 47. Looking at grammar.** (Charts 10-8 and 10-9)
Complete the sentences with the verbs in parentheses. Give short answers to questions where necessary.

1. A: (*you, have*) _____*Do you have*_____ a car?

   B: No, I _____*don't*_____. I (*take*) _____*take*_____ the bus to work every day.

2. A: (*you, walk*) _____ to work yesterday?

   B: No, I _____. I (*ride*) _____ my motorcycle.

3. A: (you, be) _____ in class tomorrow?

   B: Yes, I _____. But I (be, not) _____ in class the day after tomorrow.

4. A: Where (you, study, usually) _____?

   B: In my room.

   A: (you, go) _____ to the library to study sometimes?

   B: No. I (like, not) _____ to study at the library.

5. A: (Abby, call) _____ you last night?

   B: Yes, she _____. We (talk) _____ for a few minutes.

   A: (she, tell) _____ you about her brother, Brian?

   B: No, she _____. She (say, not) _____ anything about him. Why?

   A: Brian (be) _____ in an accident.

   B: That's too bad. What happened?

   A: A dog (run) _____ in front of his bike. He (see, not) _____ a truck next to him, and he (hit) _____ it. It was an unfortunate accident.

   B: (he, be) _____ in the hospital now?

   A: No, he _____. He (be) _____ at home.

□ **Exercise 48. Check your knowledge.** (Chapter 10)
Correct the mistakes.

       will you
1. When ~~you will~~ come?

2. Is Kiril will go to work tomorrow?

3. Will Gary to meet us for dinner tomorrow?

4. We went to a movie last evening.

5. What time you are going to come tomorrow?

6. My sister is going to meet me at the airport. My brother won't to be there.

7. Mr. Pang will sells his business and retires next year.

8. Do you will be in Venezuela next year?

9. I saw Jim three day ago.

10. *Formal written English:* I'm gonna graduate with a degree in chemistry.

❑ **Exercise 49. Listening, reading, writing, and speaking.** (Chapter 10)

Part I. Listen to the play. Then take turns reading the roles. Look at new vocabulary with your teacher first.

Jack and the Beanstalk

NARRATOR:	Once upon a time* there was a boy named Jack. He lived with his mother in a small village.
MOTHER:	We are very poor. We have no money. Our cow has no milk.
JACK:	What are we going to do?
MOTHER:	You'll go to the market and sell the cow.
NARRATOR:	Jack left his home and met an old man on the road.
OLD MAN:	I will buy your cow. I will pay you with beans. Here, these are magic beans.
NARRATOR:	Jack took the beans home to his mother.
MOTHER:	You stupid boy. We have nothing now. We are going to die.
NARRATOR:	She threw the beans out the window. The next morning, Jack woke up and saw a huge beanstalk outside his window. It went into the clouds. He decided to climb it. At the top, he saw a castle. Inside the castle, there lived a giant and his wife. He went into the castle.
WIFE:	What are you doing? My husband likes to eat boys for breakfast. You need to hide or he will eat you.
JACK:	I'm so scared. Please help me.

Do you know these words?

village	oven
magic beans	bones
giant	axe

a castle

a beanstalk

---

once upon a time = a long time ago

WIFE: Here, climb inside the oven. After breakfast, my husband will fall asleep.

GIANT: Fee-Fi-Fo-Fum,*
I smell the blood of an Englishman.
If he's alive or if he's dead,
I'll use his bones to make my bread.

Hmm. I smell a boy. Wife, are you going to feed me a boy for breakfast?

WIFE: No, I think the smell is the boy from last week. Here's your breakfast.

NARRATOR: The giant ate, counted his gold coins, and soon fell asleep. Jack got out of the oven, took a few gold coins, climbed down the beanstalk, and ran to his mother.

MOTHER: Oh, Jack. You saved us. Now we have money for food. But you are not going to go back to the castle. The giant will eat you.

NARRATOR: But Jack wanted more money. Soon he climbed the beanstalk. Again the giant's wife hid Jack in the oven. The giant had a hen. It laid golden eggs. After the giant fell asleep, Jack stole the hen.

a harp

a hen

MOTHER: What will we do with a hen? Why didn't you bring more gold coins? Jack, you have no sense.

JACK: Wait, mother. The hen is going to lay a golden egg. Watch.

NARRATOR: The hen laid a golden egg.

MOTHER: Oh, you wonderful boy! We will be rich.

NARRATOR: But Jack wanted more from the giant, so he went up the beanstalk one more time. This time, a golden harp was playing. It made beautiful music. Soon the giant went to sleep, and Jack took the harp. The giant heard a noise and woke up.

GIANT: I will catch you and eat you alive.

---

*Fee-Fi-Fo-Fum = words with no meaning. They help the second line rhyme.

NARRATOR: The giant ran after Jack. Jack climbed down the beanstalk. The giant followed. Jack took an axe and chopped down the stalk. The giant fell.

GIANT: Ahhhhhhhhhh!

JACK: The giant is dead.

MOTHER: Now we are safe. The harp will give us beautiful music. My sadness will go away. Our lives will be happy. You saved us!

NARRATOR: And they lived happily ever after.

Part II. Work in small groups. Complete the play below. Jack is now Jill. The giant is now a dragon. Make the lines silly, funny, or just different.

Jill and the Dragon

NARRATOR: Once upon a time there was a girl named Jill. She lived with her mother in a small village.

MOTHER: We are very poor. We have no money for food.

JILL: _____

MOTHER: _____

NARRATOR: Jill left her home and met a/an _____ on the road.

_____ : _____

NARRATOR: Jill took the _____ home to her mother.

MOTHER: _____

NARRATOR: She threw the _____ out the window. The next morning, Jill woke up and saw a huge _____ outside her window. It went into the clouds. She decided to climb it. At the top, she saw a castle. Inside the castle, there lived a fire-breathing dragon and his wife. He owned all the gold in the kingdom. Jill went into the castle.

a dragon

WIFE: _____

JILL: _____

WIFE: _____

DRAGON: _____

NARRATOR: Jill ran down the _____ with a few gold coins in her hands. Her clothes were a little burned, but she was safe.

MOTHER: _____

JILL: _____

NARRATOR: The next morning, Jill climbed up the _____ again. She carried a sack with her.

DRAGON: _____

WIFE: _____

DRAGON: _____

NARRATOR: Jill escaped from the castle with the sack full of gold coins. She ran down the _____. The dragon tried to catch her. He jumped on the _____, but when he breathed, the _____ caught on fire. It burned to the ground. The dragon fell and died.

JILL: _____

MOTHER: _____

NARRATOR: And they lived happily ever after.

Part III. Editing check: Work individually or change papers with a partner. Check (✓) for the following:

1. ____ capital letter at the beginning of each sentence

2. ____ period at the end of each sentence

3. ____ use of **will** or **be going to** for a future activity

4. ____ use of past verbs for past activities

5. ____ correct use of time expressions with present, past, and future

6. ____ correct spelling (use a dictionary or spell-check)

Part IV. OPTION 1: Practice and perform your play for the class.

OPTION 2: Practice and perform "Jack and the Beanstalk" for the class.

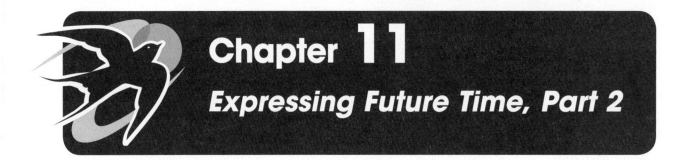

Chapter 11

Expressing Future Time, Part 2

❑ **Exercise 1. Warm-up.** (Chart 11-1)
Which two sentences have the same meaning?

1. Jon **might** change jobs.
2. Jon **will** change jobs.
3. Jon **may** change jobs.

11-1 *May/Might* vs. *Will*

(a) It **may rain** *tomorrow*. (b) Anita **may be** at home *now*.	**May** + verb (base form) expresses a possibility in the future, as in (a), or a present possibility, as in (b).
(c) It **might rain** *tomorrow*. (d) Anita **might be** at home *now*.	**Might** has the same meaning as **may**. Examples (a) and (c) have the same meaning. Examples (b) and (d) have the same meaning.
(e) Tom **will be** at the meeting *tomorrow*. (f) Ms. Lee **may/might be** at the meeting *tomorrow*.	In (e): The speaker uses **will** because he feels sure about Tom's presence at the meeting tomorrow. In (f): The speaker uses **may/might** to say, "I don't know if Ms. Lee will be at the meeting, but it is possible."
(g) Ms. Lee **may/might not be** at the meeting *tomorrow*.	Negative form: **may/might** + **not** NOTE: Examples (f) and (g) have essentially the same meaning: Ms. Lee may or may not be at the meeting tomorrow.
INCORRECT: *Ms. Lee may will be at the meeting tomorrow.* INCORRECT: *Ms. Lee might will be at the meeting tomorrow.*	**May** and **might** are <u>not</u> used with **will**.

Exercise 2. Looking at grammar. (Chart 11-1)
Complete the sentences. Use **will** or **won't** if you are sure. Use **may** or **might** if you are not sure.

1. I _____ be in class next Monday.

   → *I **will be** in class next Monday.* = You're sure.

   → *I **will not** (**won't**) **be** in class next Monday.* = You're sure.

   → *I **may/might be** in class next Monday.* OR

   → *I **may/might not be** in class next Monday.* = It's possible, but you're not sure.

2. I _____ eat breakfast tomorrow morning.

3. I _____ be in class tomorrow.

4. I _____ get a text from a friend of mine tomorrow.

5. I _____ watch TV for a little while after dinner tonight.

6. We _____ have a grammar test tomorrow.

7. I _____ eat dinner at a restaurant tonight.

8. It _____ be cloudy tomorrow.

9. The sun _____ rise tomorrow morning.

10. I _____ choose a career in music after I finish school.

11. The population of the earth _____ continue to grow.

12. Cities _____ become more and more crowded.

13. We _____ live on other planets.

❏ **Exercise 3. Let's talk: small groups.** (Chart 11-1)

Work in small groups. Take turns completing the sentences about yourself and other people in the list.

I	a friend
you (name of a classmate)	a world leader
your teacher	a movie star
a member of your family	a famous athlete

1. In five years, _____ will _____.

2. Next year, _____ may not _____.

3. _____ might _____ tomorrow.

4. _____ might or might not _____ next week.

5. _____ won't _____ in 2025.

6. _____ might not _____ tomorrow.

7. Next year, _____ won't _____.

8. In 20 years, _____ may _____.

9. Next week, _____ may or may not _____.

10. _____ will _____ in a few years.

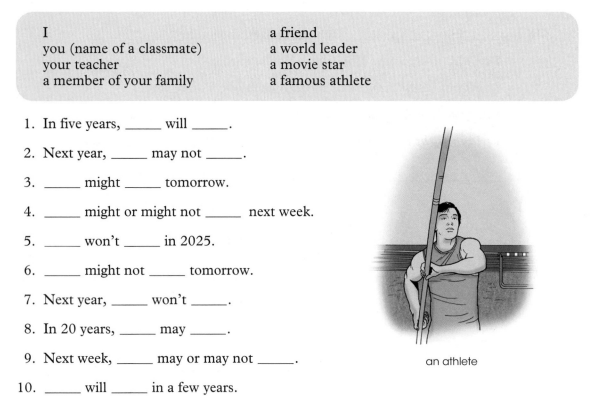

an athlete

❏ **Exercise 4. Writing and speaking.** (Chart 11-1)

Write two paragraphs. Use the given words in the paragraphs below. Use your own paper.

Paragraph 1: Write about your activities *yesterday*.
Paragraph 2: Write about your activities *tomorrow*. Include activities you **will** do and activities you **may** or **might** do.

Then show your paragraphs to a partner. Your partner will share some of your activities with the class.

PARAGRAPH 1.

I got up at _____ yesterday morning. After that, _____. Around _____ o'clock, _____. Later _____. At _____ o'clock, _____. Then _____. _____ a little later. Then at _____ o'clock _____.

PARAGRAPH 2.

I'm going to get up at _____ tomorrow morning. Then _____. After that, _____. Around _____ o'clock, _____. Later _____. At _____ o'clock, _____. Next, _____. _____ a little later. Then at _____ o'clock, _____.

Which answers are true for you? What do you notice about *may* and *maybe* in sentence c.?

1. *Tomorrow morning, . . .*
   a. I will go to school early.
   b. I won't go to school early.
   c. I may go to school early.

2. *Tomorrow night, . . .*
   a. I will go to the library.
   b. I won't go to the library.
   c. maybe I will go to the library.

11-2 *Maybe* (One Word) vs. *May Be* (Two Words)

(a) A: Will Jamal be in class tomorrow? B: I don't know. **Maybe. Maybe Jamal will be** in class tomorrow, and **maybe he won't**.	The adverb **maybe** (one word) means "possibly."
(b) | **Maybe** | Jamal | will be | here. adverb subject verb	**Maybe** comes in front of a subject and verb.
(c) | Jamal | **may be** | here tomorrow. subject verb	**May be** (two words) is used as the verb of a sentence.

❑ **Exercise 6. Looking at grammar.** (Chart 11-2)

Find the sentences where *maybe* is used as an adverb and where *may* is used as part of the verb. Choose the correct answer.

1. Maybe it will rain tomorrow.   (adverb)   verb

2. It may rain tomorrow.   adverb   (verb)

3. We may go to the art museum tomorrow.   adverb   verb

4. Maybe Jessica will come with us.   adverb   verb

5. She may have a day off tomorrow.   adverb   verb

6. It's cold and cloudy today. It may be cold and cloudy tomorrow.   adverb   verb

7. Maybe the weather will be warm and sunny this weekend.   adverb   verb

❏ **Exercise 7. Looking at grammar.** (Chart 11-2)
Complete the sentences with *maybe* or *may be*.

1. A: I _____*may be*_____ a little late tonight.

   B: That's okay. I won't worry about you.

2. A: Will you be here by seven o'clock?

   B: It's hard to say. _____*Maybe*_____ I'll be a little late.

3. A: It _____ cold tomorrow.

   B: That's okay. Let's go to the beach anyway.

4. A: Will the plane be on time?

   B: I think so, but it _____ a few minutes late.

5. A: Do you want to go to the park tomorrow?

   B: Sure. That sounds like fun.

   A: Let's talk to Carlos too. _____ he would like to go with us.

6. A: Where's Mr. Callis?

   B: Look in Room 506 down the hall. I think he _____ there.

   A: No, he's not there. I just looked in Room 506.

   B: _____ he's in Room 508.

❏ **Exercise 8. Let's talk.** (Chart 11-2)
Work in groups or as a class. The group leader or your teacher will ask you questions.
Answer them by using *I don't know* + *maybe* or *may/might*. If you work in groups,
choose a new leader where indicated.

Example:
TEACHER/LEADER: What are you going to do tonight?
　　　　STUDENT: I don't know. Maybe I'll watch TV. / I may watch TV. / I might
　　　　　　　　watch TV.

1. What are you going to do tonight?
2. What are you going to do tomorrow?
3. What are you going to do after class today?
4. What are you going to do this weekend?
5. What are you going to do this evening?

Choose a new leader.
6. Who is going to go shopping tomorrow? What are you going to buy?
7. Who is going to go out to eat tonight? Where are you going to go?
8. Who is going to watch TV tonight? What are you going to watch?
9. Who is going to get married? When?

Choose a new leader.

10. Who is going to leave class early? Why?

11. Is it going to rain tomorrow? What is the weather going to be like tomorrow?

12. Who is planning to go on a vacation? Where are you going to go?

13. Who wants to have a pet? What kind of pet are you going to get?

❏ **Exercise 9. Looking at grammar.** (Chart 11-2)
Rewrite the sentences. Use the words in parentheses.

1. Maybe I will study.

   a. (*might*) _____ I might study. _____

   b. (*may*) _____ I may study. _____

2. The teacher might give a test.

   a. (*maybe*) _____

   b. (*may*) _____

3. Maybe Natalie will be home early.

   a (*may*) _____

   b. (*might*) _____

4. She might be late.

   a. (*maybe*) _____

   b. (*may*) _____

5. It may rain tomorrow.

   a. (*maybe*) _____

   b. (*might*) _____

❏ **Exercise 10. Listening.** (Chart 11-2)
Listen to the sentences. Choose the use of *may* that you hear.

Example: You will hear: Maybe I'll see you tomorrow.
         You will choose: (Maybe)   *May* + verb

1. *maybe*	*may* + verb		5. *Maybe*	*May* + verb
2. *maybe*	*may* + verb		6. *Maybe*	*May* + verb
3. *Maybe*	*May* + verb		7. *maybe*	*may* + verb
4. *maybe*	*may* + verb		8. *Maybe*	*May* + verb

❑ **Exercise 11. Looking at grammar.** (Chart 11-2)
Answer the questions. Use *maybe* or *may/might*.

1. A: Is Anthony going to come to the party?
   B: I don't know. _____*Maybe*_____ .

2. A: What are you going to do tomorrow?
   B: I don't know. I _____*may / might*_____ go swimming.

3. A: Are Lilly and James going to get married?
   B: _____. Who knows?

4. A: Where is Robert?
   B: I don't know. He _____ be at his office.

5. A: Where is Robert?
   B: I don't know. _____ he's at his office.

6. A: I'd like to have a pet.
   B: What kind of pet would you like to get?
   A: I'm not sure. _____ I'll get
      a canary. Or _____ I'll get a snake.
      I _____ get a fish. Or I
      _____ get a turtle.
   B: What's wrong with a cat or dog?

a canary

❑ **Exercise 12. Let's talk: pairwork.** (Charts 11-1 and 11-2)
Work with a partner. Use the phrases below to tell your partner about your activities
tomorrow. Use *will/won't, going to/not going to, maybe, may,* and *might*.

Example: go to a movie / go shopping
PARTNER A: I'm not going to go to a movie tomorrow. OR I might go shopping.
PARTNER B: I might go to a movie. OR Maybe I'll go shopping.

1. wake up early / sleep in
2. eat a big breakfast / eat a small breakfast
3. stay home / go to school
4. get some exercise in the afternoon / take a nap in the afternoon
5. do my homework in the evening / watch TV in the evening
6. eat an ice cream cone / eat vegetables
7. cook dinner / eat out
8. shop online / shop at a store

an ice
cream cone

9. clean my house (apartment, bedroom, car, kitchen) / read a book

10. visit a friend / visit a social networking site

❏ **Exercise 13. Listening.** (Charts 11-1 and 11-2)

Listen to each sentence. Choose the sentence that has the same meaning as the sentence you hear.

Example: You will hear: I might be absent tomorrow.
    You will choose: (a.) Maybe I will be absent.   b. I'm going to be absent.

1. a. Our plans will change.
   b. Our plans might change.

2. a. It is going to rain.
   b. Maybe it will rain.

3. a. We may finish this grammar book soon.
   b. We will finish this grammar book soon.

4. a. Maybe Henry will get good news tomorrow.
   b. Henry is going to get good news tomorrow.

5. a. The class may start on time.
   b. The class is going to start on time.

❏ **Exercise 14. Let's talk: pairwork.** (Charts 11-1 and 11-2)

Work with a partner. Check (✓) the boxes that describe your activities tomorrow. Show your answers to your partner. She/He will make sentences about you using *may*, *might*, or *maybe*. Share some of them with the class.

Example: eat lunch / go shopping, etc.
Possible sentences: (*to your partner*) You may eat lunch. You won't go shopping. Etc.
            (*to the class*) She/He may eat lunch. She/He won't go shopping. Etc.

ACTIVITY	YES	NO	MAYBE
1. eat lunch			
2. go shopping			
3. send some emails			
4. watch TV			
5. talk on the phone			
6. play soccer			
7. read an English language newspaper			
8. look up information on the Internet			
9. have dinner with friends			
10. chat online			

❑ **Exercise 15. Warm-up.** (Chart 11-3)
<u>Underline</u> the time word in each sentence. What tense is used in the red clause? Does the clause have present or future meaning?

   1. Before I go on vacation next week, I'm going to clean my apartment.

   2. When I get home next month, my apartment will be clean.

11-3 Future Time Clauses with *Before, After,* and *When*

(a) *Before Ann **goes** to work tomorrow,* she will eat breakfast. INCORRECT: *Before Ann will go to work tomorrow, she will eat breakfast.* INCORRECT: *Before Ann is going to go to work tomorrow, she will eat breakfast.*	In (a): ***Before Ann goes to work tomorrow*** = a future time clause;* ***she will eat breakfast*** = main clause. A future time clause uses the SIMPLE PRESENT TENSE. *Will* OR *be going to* is used in the main clause.
(b) I'm going to finish my homework *after I **eat** dinner tonight.* (c) *When I **go** to New York next week,* I'm going to stay at the Hilton Hotel.	In (b): ***after I eat dinner tonight*** = a future time clause In (c): ***When I go to New York next week*** = a future time clause Notice: A comma follows a time clause when it comes at the beginning of a sentence.

*See Chart 9-7, p. 284, for more information about time clauses.

❑ **Exercise 16. Looking at grammar.** (Chart 11-3)
<u>Underline</u> the time clauses.

   1. <u>After I get home tonight</u>, I'm going to email my parents.

   2. Mr. Masri will finish his report before he leaves the office today.

   3. I'll get some fresh fruit when I go to the grocery store tomorrow.

   4. Before I go to bed tonight, I'm going to read a story to my little brother.

   5. I'm going to look for a job with a computer company after I graduate next year.

❑ **Exercise 17. Looking at grammar.** (Chart 11-3)
Complete the sentences with the words in parentheses. Use ***be going to*** for the future.

   1. Before I (*go*) _____*go*_____ to bed tonight, I (*watch*) _____*am going to watch*_____ my favorite show on TV.

   2. I (*buy*) _____ a new coat when I (*go*) _____ shopping tomorrow.

   3. After I (*finish*) _____ my homework this evening, I (*text*) _____ _____ my friends.

4. When I (*see*) _____ Eduardo tomorrow, I (*ask*) _____

_____ him to join us for dinner this weekend.

5. Before I (*buy*) _____ my plane ticket to Australia, I (*check*) _____

_____ websites for cheap airfares.

❏ **Exercise 18. Looking at grammar.** **(Chart 11-3)**
Write "1" before the first action and "2" before the second. Then write two sentences: one with **before** and one with **after**. Use a form of **be going to** in the main clause.

1. __1__ I brush my teeth.

__2__ I go to bed.

a. ___*I'm going to brush my teeth before I go to bed.* OR_____

___*Before I go to bed, I'm going to brush my teeth.*_____

b. ___*After I brush my teeth, I'm going to go to bed.* OR_____

___*I'm going to go to bed after I brush my teeth.*_____

2. ____ I go to sleep.

____ I turn off my cell phone.

a. _____

b. _____

3. ____ I spell-check the words.

____ I turn in my essay.

a. _____

b. _____

4. ____ The passengers get on the airplane.

____ The passengers go through security.

a. _____

b. _____

❑ **Exercise 19. Let's talk: class activity.** (Chart 11-3)
Your teacher will ask you questions. Give complete answers using time clauses. Close your book for this activity.

Example:
TEACHER: Who's going to go shopping later today?
STUDENT A: (*raises his/her hand*)
TEACHER: What are you going to do after you go shopping?
STUDENT A: After I go shopping, I'm going to go home. OR
     I'm going to go home after I go shopping.
TEACHER: (*to Student B*) What is (*Student A*) going to do after he/she goes shopping?
STUDENT B: After (*Student A*) goes shopping, he/she is going to go home. OR
     (*Student A*) is going to go home after he/she goes shopping.

1. Who's going to study tonight? What are you going to do after you study tonight?

2. Who else is going to study tonight? What are you going to do before you study tonight?

3. Who's going to watch TV tonight? What are you going to do before you watch TV?

4. Who else is going to watch TV tonight? What are you going to do after you watch TV?

5. (. . .), what are you going to do tomorrow? What are you going to do before you ____ tomorrow? What are you going to do after you ____ tomorrow?

6. Who's going out of town soon? Where are you going? What are you going to do when you go to (*name of place*)?

7. Who's going to eat dinner tonight? What are you going to do before you eat dinner? What are you going to do after you eat dinner? What are you going to have for dinner?

8. (. . .), what time are you going to get home today? What are you going to do before you get home? What are you going to do when you get home? What are you going to do after you get home?

❑ **Exercise 20. Let's talk.** (Chart 11-3)
Imagine that one day you will speak English fluently. What will you do? What won't you do? Make statements with **will** and **won't**. Work with a partner, in groups, or as a class.

When I speak English fluently, I . . .

1. need a dictionary.

2. think in English.

3. feel relaxed with native speakers.

4. dream in English.

5. have an accent.

6. translate from my language.

7. speak with my friends in English.

8. speak with my family in English.

❑ **Exercise 21. Speaking and writing: pairwork.** (Chart 11-3)

Part I. Read the writing sample and think about your own future. What are some special things that you would like to do in your life?

> In 2020, Hans is going to climb Mt. Everest. He's going to train for a couple of years first. Then he's going to climb with a group of people. When he gets to the top, he's going to put a flag from his country in the snow.
>
> In 2025, Hans is going to swim with dolphins. He is going to have an underwater video camera with him. After he takes the video, he will make a short movie for family and friends.

Write your plans in the chart. Also, write down the year. Then give it to your partner.

YEAR	ACTIVITY

Part II. Write about your partner's plans. Try to include some time clauses beginning with ***when, after,*** and ***before.*** Ask your partner questions about the activities to get more information.

❑ **Exercise 22. Warm-up.** (Chart 11-4)

Choose the correct verbs.

A: What are you going to do next weekend?

B: If I   have / will have   time, I   help / will help   you move to your new dorm room.

A: Wow! Great!

11-4 Clauses with *If*

(a)	**If it rains tomorrow,** | we will stay home. | *if*-clause main clause	An *if*-clause begins with **if** and has a subject and a verb. An *if*-clause can come before or after a main clause.
(b)	| We will stay home | **if it rains tomorrow.** | main clause *if*-clause	Notice: A comma follows an *if*-clause when it comes at the beginning of a sentence.
(c)	**If it *rains*** *tomorrow,* we won't go on a picnic.	The SIMPLE PRESENT is used in the *if*-clause to express future time. ***Will*** or
(d)	I'm going to buy a new car next year ***if I have*** enough money. **If I *don't have*** enough money next year for a new car, I'm going to buy a used car.	***be going to*** is used in the main clause.

☐ **Exercise 23. Looking at grammar.** (Chart 11-4)

Choose the correct verbs.

SITUATION: Andrew is applying for a new job in New York City.

1. If Andrew   gets / will get   the job, he is going to move there.

2. If he   moves / is going to move   there, he is going to rent an apartment.

3. If he   rents / is going to rent   an apartment, he is going to need extra money.

4. If he   needs / will need   extra money, his parents will loan him some.

5. If his parents   loan / will loan   him money, he will be very grateful.

☐ **Exercise 24. Let's talk: pairwork.** (Chart 11-4)

Work with a partner. Ask and answer questions.

    Partner A: Ask a question that begins with ***What are you going to do . . . ?***
              Your book is open.
    Partner B: Answer the question. Include the *if*-clause in your answer.
              Your book is closed.

Example: . . . if the weather is nice tomorrow?
PARTNER A: What are you going to do if the weather is nice tomorrow?
PARTNER B: If the weather is nice tomorrow, I'm going to sit outside in the sun. OR
              I'm going to sit outside in the sun if the weather is nice tomorrow.

1. . . . if the weather is cold tomorrow?

2. . . . if the weather is hot tomorrow?

3. . . . if you don't understand a question that I ask you?

4. . . . if you don't feel well tomorrow?

5. . . . if you go to (*name of a place in this city*) tomorrow?

Change roles.

6. . . . if it snows tonight?

7. . . . if you're hungry after class today?

8. . . . if you don't study tonight?

9. . . . if you lose your grammar book?

10. . . . if someone steals your (*name of a thing: bike, wallet, etc.*)?

❏ **Exercise 25. Looking at grammar.** (Chart 11-4)

Complete the sentences with the words in parentheses. Use *be going to* or *will* for the future.

1. If Malik (*be*) _____*is*_____ in class tomorrow, I (*ask*) _____*am going to / will ask*_____ him to join us for coffee after class.

2. If the weather (*be*) _____ nice tomorrow, I (*go*) _____ _____ to Central Park with my friends.

3. I (*stay, not*) _____ home tomorrow if the weather (*be*) _____ nice.

4. If I (*feel, not*) _____ well tomorrow, I (*go, not*) _____ _____ to work.

5. Masako (*stay*) _____ in bed tomorrow if she (*feel, not*) _____ well.

6. We (*stay*) _____ with my aunt and uncle if we (*go*) _____ _____ to Miami next week.

7. If my friends (*be*) _____ busy tomorrow, I (*go*) _____ to a movie by myself.

❏ **Exercise 26. Listening.** (Chart 11-4)

Listen to the questions. Answer each question in a complete sentence. Remember, *going to* may sound like *gonna*.

1. _____

2. _____

3. _____

4. _____

❏ **Exercise 27. Reading and speaking.** (Charts 11-1 → 11-4)

Part I. Read the story and answer the questions. Look at new vocabulary with your teacher first.

Life in 100 Years

In December of 1900, *Ladies Home Journal,* an American magazine, published an article titled "What May Happen in the Next Hundred Years." There were 29 predictions about life in the year 2000. Below are some of them.

> *Do you know these words?*
>
> magazine
> prediction
> ambulance
> tunnel

Cars will be cheaper and stronger than horses. They will do the work of two horses or more. Police, ambulance drivers, and street cleaners will use cars instead of horses. People won't see horses on the streets.

Big cities won't have streetcars. In the future, if people need to go somewhere, they will travel below or high above the ground. Subways and tunnels will have moving stairways, and they will carry people up or down.

There will be no C, X, or Q in the English alphabet because these sounds are not necessary. In the future, people will spell by sound. First, newspapers will do this. After people see this change, they will do the same.

A final prediction: English will be the number one language in the world and Russian will be number two.

1. Which predictions came true?
2. Which ones did not?
3. Are there any predictions you think are silly or strange?

Part II. Work in small groups. Make some predictions for 100 years from now. Use *will, may, maybe,* or *might.*

❏ **Exercise 28. Warm-up.** (Chart 11-5)
Choose the correct time word for each sentence.

1. Before I go to the beach, I put on sunscreen.   every day   tomorrow

2. Before I go to the beach, I am going to put on sunscreen.   every day   tomorrow

11-5 Expressing Future and Habitual Present with Time Clauses and *If*-Clauses

FUTURE	(a) After Kate **gets** to work today, she **is going to have** / **will have** a cup of coffee.	Example (a) expresses a specific activity in the future. The SIMPLE PRESENT is used in the time clause. *Be going to* or *will* is used in the main clause.
HABITUAL PRESENT	(b) After Kate **gets** to work (every day), she always **has** a cup of coffee.	Example (b) expresses habitual activities, so the SIMPLE PRESENT is used in both the time clause and the main clause.
FUTURE	(c) If it **rains** tomorrow, I **am going to** / **will wear** my raincoat to school.	Example (c) expresses a specific activity in the future. The SIMPLE PRESENT is used in the if-clause. *Be going to* or *will* is used in the main clause.
HABITUAL PRESENT	(d) If it **rains**, I **wear** my raincoat.	Example (d) expresses habitual activities, so the SIMPLE PRESENT is used in both the if-clause and the main clause.

❏ **Exercise 29. Looking at grammar.** (Chart 11-5)
Decide the meaning for each sentence: present habit or future activity.

1. Before I eat dinner, I set the table. (present habit)   future activity

2. Before I eat dinner, I'm going to set the table.   present habit   future activity

3. When I play video games for too long, I get a headache.   present habit   future activity

4. If Jim takes the subway, he gets home quickly.   present habit   future activity

5. Before the movie starts, I'll turn off my cell phone.   present habit   future activity

6. When I go to bed, I turn off my phone.   present habit   future activity

❏ **Exercise 30. Looking at grammar.** (Chart 11-5)
Complete the sentences with the words in parentheses. Use **be going to** for the future.

1. When we (*go*) _____ to Quebec, we (*stay, usually*) _____

   _____ with my in-laws.

2. When I (*go*) _____ to Quebec next week, we (*stay*) _____

   _____ with my in-laws.

3. I (*have*) _____ some strong coffee before I (*go*) _____ to class today.

4. I (*have, usually*) _____ some strong coffee before I (*go*) _____ to class.

5. I'm often tired in the evening after a long day at work. If I (*be*) _____ tired in the evening, I (*stay, usually*) _____ home and (*go*) _____ to bed early.

6. If I (*be*) _____ tired this evening, I (*stay*) _____ home and (*go*) _____ to bed early.

7. After I (*get*) _____ home in the evening, I (*sit, usually*) _____ _____ on the couch with my laptop and (*look at*) _____ newspapers online.

8. After I (*get*) _____ home tonight, I (*sit*) _____ on the couch with my laptop and (*look at*) _____ newspapers online.

9. Before the teacher (*walk*) _____ into the room every day, there (*be*) _____ a lot of noise in the classroom.

10. People (*yawn, often*) _____ and (*stretch*) _____ when they (*wake*) _____ up.

11. Simon (*close*) _____ all the windows in his apartment before he (*turn*) _____ on the air-conditioning.

12. When I (*go*) _____ to Taiwan next month, I (*stay*) _____ _____ with my friend Mr. Chu. After I (*leave*) _____ Taiwan, I (*go*) _____ to Hong Kong.

13. Ms. Tan (*go*) _____ to Hong Kong often. When she (*be*) _____ there, she (*like*) _____ to take the ferry across the bay, but she (*take*) _____ the subway under the bay if she (*be*) _____ in a hurry.

Exercise 31. Looking at grammar: small groups. (Chart 11-5)

Work in small groups. Match each word or phrase in Column A with a phrase in Column B. Take turns making a sentence that expresses habitual activity for each situation. After you are finished, write a sentence for each one.

Column A

What does Steven do if he . . .

1. fails a test? __c__
2. is hungry? ____
3. is tired? ____
4. gets a mosquito bite? ____
5. oversleeps? ____
6. gets a sore throat? ____

Column B

a. takes a nap
b. skips breakfast
✓c. studies more
d. eats a piece of fruit
e. drinks tea with honey
f. tries not to scratch it

1. _____If he fails a test, he studies more._____
2. _____
3. _____
4. _____
5. _____
6. _____

Exercise 32. Listening. (Chart 11-5)

Listen to each sentence and choose the correct completion.

Example: You will hear: Before I go to bed every night,
            You will choose: (a.) I watch TV.   b. I'm going to watch TV.

1. a. I get a good night's sleep.   b. I'll get a good night's sleep.
2. a. I do my homework.   b. I'll do my homework.
3. a. I go shopping.   b. I'll go shopping.
4. a. I exercise.   b. I'll exercise.
5. a. I call my parents.   b. I'll call my parents.
6. a. I'm happy.   b. I'll be happy.
7. a. I know a lot of grammar.   b. I'll know a lot of grammar.

❏ **Exercise 33. Looking at grammar.** (Chart 11-5)
Complete the sentences with your own words.

1. Before I go home tonight, _____.

2. Before I go home, I usually _____.

3. I'm going to _____ tomorrow after I _____.

4. When I go to _____, I'm going to _____.

5. When I go to _____, I always _____.

6. If the weather _____ tomorrow, I _____.

7. If the weather _____ tomorrow, _____

   you going to _____?

8. I'll _____ if I _____.

9. After I _____ tonight, I _____.

10. Do you _____ after you _____?

❏ **Exercise 34. Warm-up.** (Chart 11-6)
Read the questions and answers. Which conversation asks, "What is your job"?

CONVERSATION 1. A: What do you do every day?   B: I deliver the mail.

CONVERSATION 2. A: What did you do yesterday?   B: I delivered the mail.

CONVERSATION 3. A: What do you do?   B: I'm a mail carrier.

11-6 Using *What* + a Form of *Do*

PRESENT		In (a) and (b): ***What*** + a form of ***do*** is used to ask about activities.
(a) *What **do** you **do** every day?*	→ I *work* every day.	
(b) *What **are** you **doing** right now?*	→ I'm *studying English*.	
(c) *What **do** you **do**?*	→ I'm *a teacher*.	
PAST		In (c): *What do you do?* means "What kind of work do you do?" OR "What is your job?"
(d) *What **did** you **do** yesterday?*	→ I *went to school* yesterday.	
FUTURE		
(e) *What **are** you **going to do** tomorrow?*	→ I'm *going to go downtown* tomorrow.	
(f) *What **will** we **do** if it rains tomorrow?*	→ We'*ll stay home* if it rains tomorrow.	

❏ **Exercise 35. Let's talk: class activity.** (Chart 11-6)

Your teacher will ask you questions. Answer them in complete sentences. Close your book for this activity.

Example:
TEACHER: What do you do when you get up in the morning?
STUDENT A: When I get up in the morning, I eat breakfast.
STUDENT B: I listen to music when I get up in the morning.

1. What do you do when you get up in the morning?
2. What are you going to do when you get up tomorrow morning?
3. What do you usually do before you eat breakfast?
4. What are you going to do after class today?
5. What are you going to do when you get home?
6. What do you usually do after you get home?
7. What do you like to do if the weather is nice?
8. What are you going to do if the weather is nice tomorrow?

❏ **Exercise 36. Looking at grammar.** (Chart 11-6)

Make questions for the given answer using a form of *do*.

1. _____*What does she do?*_____ Nancy's an accountant.

2. _____ We're students.

3. _____ I'm a doctor.

4. _____ They're janitors.

an accountant

5. _____ He's a server at a restaurant.

a server

a plumber

6. _____ She's a plumber.

7. _____ You're a sales manager.

8. _____ William and I are taxi drivers.

❏ **Exercise 37. Let's talk: pairwork.** (Chart 11-6)
Work with a partner. Ask your partner questions. Use **What** + *a form of do* with the given time expression. You can look at your book before you speak. When you speak, look at your partner.

Example: yesterday
PARTNER A (*book open*): What did you do yesterday?
PARTNER B (*book closed*): I read a newspaper yesterday.

1. last night	*Change roles.*
2. every day	8. tomorrow evening
3. right now	9. last Saturday
4. tomorrow	10. next Saturday
5. yesterday afternoon	11. this morning
6. tomorrow morning	12. this afternoon
7. every morning	13. tonight
	14. next week

❏ **Exercise 38. Looking at grammar.** (Chart 11-6)
Complete the sentences with the words in parentheses. Use **be going to** for the future.

1. A: What (*you, do*) _____*do you do*_____ every Friday?

   B: I (*come*) _____*come*_____ to class.

2. A: What (*you, do*) _____ last Friday?

   B: I (*come*) _____ to class.

3. A: What (*you, do*) _____ next Friday?

   B: I (*come*) _____ to class.

4. A: What (*you, do*) _____ yesterday evening?

   B: I (*chat*) _____ online with my friends.

5. A: What (*you, do*) _____ every evening?

   B: I (*chat*) _____ online with my friends.

6. A: What (*you, do*) _____ tomorrow evening?

   B: I (*chat*) _____ online with my friends.

7. A: What (*you, do*) _____ right now?

   B: I (*do*) _____ a grammar exercise.

8. A: What (*Marina, do*) _____ every morning?

   B: She (*go*) _____ to work.

9. A: What (*the students*) _____ right now?

   B: They (*work*) _____ on this exercise.

10. A: What (*they, do*) _____ in class tomorrow?

    B: They (*take*) _____ a test.

11. A: What (*Bakari, do*) _____ last night?

    B: He (*go*) _____ to a movie.

12. A: What (*the teacher, do*) _____ every day at the beginning of class?

    B: She (*put*) _____ her books on her desk, (*look*) _____ at the class, and (*say*) _____ "Good morning."

Exercise 39. Listening. (Chapters 10 and 11)

Complete the conversations with the words you hear.

1. A: _____ late for the movie?

   B: No. The movie _____ at 7:30. We have plenty of time.

2. A: What _____ for dinner?

   B: Leftovers. Is that okay?

   A: Sure, but _____ probably _____ some rice to go with them.

3. A: _____ at Jon's wedding?

   B: Yes, but I _____ there until after it _____.
   I work until noon.

   A: Great. _____ you there.

4. A: What _____? We need to deposit this check, and
   the cash machine is broken. Our account is almost empty.

   B: No problem. _____ it with me to work. There's an ATM* next
   door.

❑ **Exercise 40. Looking at grammar.** (Chapter 11)

Choose the correct completion.

1. A: Are you going to go to the baseball game tomorrow afternoon?
   B: I don't know. I ____.

   a. will   b. am going to   c. maybe   (d.) might

2. A: Are Ruth and Simon going to be at the meeting?
   B: No, they're too busy. They ____ be there.

   a. don't   b. won't   c. will   d. may

3. A: Are you going to go to the store today?
   B: No. I went there ____ Friday.

   a. yesterday   b. next   c. last   d. ago

4. A: When are you going to go to the bank?
   B: I'll go there before I ____ to the post office tomorrow morning.

   a. will go   b. go   c. went   d. am going

5. A: Why is the teacher late today?
   B: I don't know. ____ he overslept.

   a. Maybe   b. Did   c. May   d. Was

---

*ATM = automatic teller machine (also called a cash machine); it allows customers to deposit or withdraw money from
their bank.

6. A: Do you like to go to New York City?
   B: Yes. When I'm in New York, I always ____ new things to do and places to see.
      a. found   b. find   c. will find   d. finds

7. A: Is Ricardo going to talk to us this afternoon about our plans for tomorrow?
   B: No. He'll ____ us this evening.
      a. calls   b. calling   c. call   d. called

8. A: ____ are you going to do after class today?
   B: I'm going to go home.
      a. When   b. Where   c. What   d. What time

9. A: Where ____ Ivonne live before she moved into her new apartment?
   B: She lived in a dormitory at the university.
      a. did   b. does   c. is   d. was

10. A: What time ____ Paulina and Yuri going to arrive?
    B: Six.
      a. is   b. do   c. will   d. are

❏ **Exercise 41. Looking at grammar: past, present, future.**
    (Chapters 3, 4, and 8 → 11)
Complete the sentences with the words in parentheses. Use any appropriate verb form.

1. A: I (*skip*) _____ class tomorrow.
   B: Why?
   A: Why not?
   B: That's not a very good reason.

2. A: How did you get here?
   B: I (*take*) _____ a plane. I (*fly*) _____ here from Bangkok.

3. A: How do you usually get to class?
   B: I (*walk, usually*) _____, but sometimes I (*take*)
      _____ the bus.

4. A: Where's my phone? It (*be, not*) _____ in my purse. Maybe I left it on the subway.
   B: Take it easy. Your phone (*be*) _____ right here.

5. A: Where's your homework?

   B: I (*lose*) _____ it.

   A: Oh?

   B: I (*forget*) _____ it.

   A: Oh?

   B: I (*give*) _____ it to Roberto to give to you, but he (*lose*)

      _____ it.

   A: Oh?

   B: Someone (*steal*) _____ it.

   A: Oh?

   B: Well, actually I (*have, not*) _____ enough time to finish it
      last night.

   A: I see.

6. A: (*you, stay*) _____ here during vacation next week?

   B: No. I (*take*) _____ a trip to Montreal. I (*visit*)

      _____ my cousins.

   A: How long (*you, be*) _____ away?

   B: About five days.

7. A: Is Carol here?

   B: No, she (*be, not*) _____ . She (*leave*) _____ a few
      minutes ago.

   A: (*she, be*) _____ back soon?

   B: I think so.

   A: Where (*she, go*) _____ ?

   B: She (*go*) _____ to the drugstore.

❏ **Exercise 42. Check your knowledge.** (Chapter 11)
Correct the mistakes.

       is
1. If it ~~will be~~ cold tomorrow morning, my car won't start.

2. We maybe late for the concert tonight.

3. What time you are going to come tomorrow?

4. Amira will call us tonight when her plane will land.

5. Ellen may will be at the party.

6. When I'll see you tomorrow, I'll return your book to you.

7. I may don't be in class tomorrow.

8. Amin puts his books on his desk when he walked into his apartment.

9. I'll see my parents when I will return home for a visit next July.

10. What do you doing all day at work?

❏ **Exercise 43. Reading and writing.** (Chapter 11)
Part I. Read the writing sample. Look at new vocabulary with your teacher first.

snorkeling

penguins on an iceberg

Relaxation or Adventure?

I have an airline ticket in my pocket. It will take me anywhere in the world. Where will I go?

If I want a relaxing vacation, I may travel to Tahiti. Or if I want an adventure, I might travel to Antarctica. Both places have natural beauty. I want to travel to a place without many people or buildings.

Do you know these words?

adventure
windsurfing
sharks

If I go to Tahiti, I will sit on the beach in the sun. I will swim in the warm ocean. I might try windsurfing if I am not too scared. I love underwater swimming, so I will probably go snorkeling. But when I am snorkeling, I will stay away from sharks.

If I go to Antarctica, I will take all my warm clothes. There aren't any hotels, so I will probably take a tour boat to the South Pole. I definitely won't sit on a beach! When I am there, I want to see icebergs and penguins.

I'm excited about my trip. I just need to answer this question: What is more important to me right now: relaxation or adventure?

Part II. Now write your own story. Imagine someone gives you a plane ticket. You can travel anywhere in the world. Choose two places you would like to visit: one place for relaxation and one place for adventure. Use this model.

PARAGRAPH 1: Introduction
I have an airline ticket in my pocket. It will take me anywhere in the world. Where will I go?

PARAGRAPH 2: Name the two places. Choose a relaxing place and a place for adventure.
If I want a relaxing vacation, I may travel to ____. Or if I want an adventure, I might travel to ____. (Add one or two reasons.)

PARAGRAPH 3: Give details for the first place.
If I go to . . . .

PARAGRAPH 4: Give details for the second place.
If I go to . . . .

PARAGRAPH 5: Conclusion
I'm excited about my trip. I just need to answer this question: What is more important to me right now: relaxation or adventure?

Part III. Editing check: Work individually or change papers with a partner. Check (✓) for the following:

1. _____ indented paragraph

2. _____ capital letter at the beginning of each sentence

3. _____ period at the end of each sentence

4. _____ use of **will** or **be going to** for a future activity

5. _____ **might** or **may** + *base form of verb*

6. _____ **if** + *simple present tense* (for future meaning)

7. _____ correct spelling (use a dictionary or computer spell-check)

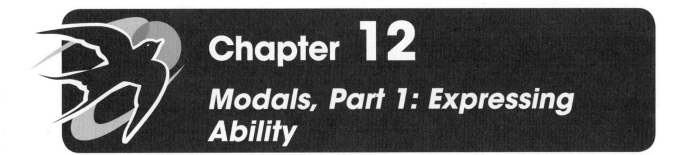

Chapter **12**

Modals, Part 1: Expressing Ability

❏ **Exercise 1. Warm-up.** (Chart 12-1)
Which answers are true for you?

1. I can / can't sing well.

2. I can / can't stand on my head.

3. I can / can't sneeze with my eyes open.

12-1 Using *Can*

(a) I have some money. I *can buy* a book. (b) We have time and money. We *can go* to a movie. (c) Tom is strong. He *can lift* the heavy box.	*Can* expresses *ability* and *possibility*.
(d) CORRECT: Yuko *can speak* English.	The base form of the main verb follows *can*. In (d): *speak* is the main verb.
(e) INCORRECT: *Yuko can to speak English.*	A main verb following *can* is NOT preceded by *to*. In (e): *to speak* is incorrect.
(f) INCORRECT: *Yuko can speaks English.*	A main verb following *can* does not have a final *-s*. In (f): *speaks* is incorrect.

(g) Alice *can not* come.
    Alice *cannot* come.
    Alice *can't* come.
	NEGATIVE
	    can + not = can not OR *cannot*
	
	CONTRACTION
	    can + not = can't

❑ **Exercise 2. Let's talk.** (Chart 12-1)
Work with a partner. Take turns making sentences from the given words. Use **can** or **can't**.

Example: A bird \ sing
→ A bird can sing.

Example: A horse \ sing
→ A horse can't sing.

1. A bird \ fly
2. A cow \ fly
3. A child \ drive a car
4. An adult \ drive a car
5. A newborn baby \ walk
6. A fish \ breathe air

7. A deaf person \ hear
8. A blind person \ see
9. An elephant \ swim
10. An elephant \ climb trees
11. A cat \ climb trees
12. A boat \ float on water

❑ **Exercise 3. Let's talk: class activity.** (Chart 12-1)
Make sentences about yourself. Begin with **I can** or **I can't**.

Example: speak Chinese
Response: I can speak Chinese. OR
I can't speak Chinese.

1. whistle
2. ride a bicycle
3. touch my ear with my elbow
4. play the piano*
5. play the guitar
6. lift a refrigerator
7. fly a plane
8. fix a flat tire

9. swim
10. float on water
11. ski
12. do advanced math in my head
13. make a paper airplane
14. sew a button on a shirt
15. wiggle my ears
16. eat with chopsticks

---

* In expressions with *play*, **the** is usually used with musical instruments: *play the piano, play the guitar, play the violin,* etc.

❏ Exercise 4. Game: small groups. (Chart 12-1)

Work in small groups. Discuss each statement. Then circle *yes* or *no*. When you are finished, check your answers with your teacher.★ The group with the most correct answers wins.

1. Some birds can't fly.   yes   no

2. Elephants can jump.   yes   no

3. Tigers can't swim.   yes   no

4. An octopus can change colors.   yes   no

5. Some fish can climb trees.   yes   no

6. Horses can't sleep when they're standing up.   yes   no

7. Turtles can't live more than 100 years.   yes   no

8. All animals can see colors.   yes   no

9. Whales can hold their breath underwater.   yes   no

a whale

an octopus

❏ Exercise 5. Warm-up: listening. (Chart 12-2)

Listen to the sentences. Which statement (a. or b.) is true for you?

1. a. I can count to 100 in English.

   b. I can't count to 100 in English.

2. a. I can't ride a bike with no hands.

   b. I can ride a bike with no hands.

★*Teacher:* See *Let's Talk: Answers,* p. 503.

12-2 Pronunciation of *Can* and *Can't*

(a) Rick *can come* to the meeting.	***Can*** is usually pronounced "kn" /kən/. It is unstressed.
(b) Mike *can't come* to the meeting.	***Can't*** is usually pronounced "kant" /kænt/ with the same vowel sound as in the word *ant*. It is stressed. You will probably not hear the /t/.*

* Sometimes native speakers also have trouble hearing the difference between *can* and *can't*.

❑ **Exercise 6. Listening.** (Chart 12-2)

Listen to each sentence. Choose the word you hear.

Example: You will hear: We can understand you.
You will choose: (can)   can't

Example: You will hear: We can't understand you.
You will choose: can   (can't)

1.	can	can't	6.	can	can't
2.	can	can't	7.	can	can't
3.	can	can't	8.	can	can't
4.	can	can't	9.	can	can't
5.	can	can't	10.	can	can't

❑ **Exercise 7. Listening.** (Chart 12-2)

Read the help-wanted ad. Then listen to Matt talk about his job skills. Decide if Matt is a good person for the job. Explain your answer.

JOB OPENING AT SMALL INTERNATIONAL HOTEL

Looking for person with the following: good typing and word-processing skills, excellent knowledge of English, friendly manner on the phone. Needs to help guests with their suitcases and be available weekends.

QUESTIONS: Is Matt a good person for this job?   yes   no
Why or why not?

❑ **Exercise 8. Warm-up.** (Chart 12-3)
Answer the questions.

1. Can you buy a hammer at a grocery store?
2. Where can you buy a hammer?

12-3 Using *Can*: Questions

(QUESTION WORD) +	*CAN* +	SUBJECT +	MAIN VERB			ANSWER
(a)	Can	you	speak	Arabic?	→	Yes, I can.
					→	No, I can't.
(b)	Can	Rosa	come	to the party?	→	Yes, she can.
					→	No, she can't.
(c) Where	can	I	buy	a hammer?	→	At a hardware store.
(d) When	can	you	help	me?	→	Tomorrow afternoon.

❑ **Exercise 9. Question practice.** (Chart 12-3)
Make yes/no questions. Give short answers.

1. A: ___Can Daria speak English?___
   B: ___Yes, she can.___ (Daria can speak English.)

2. A: ___Can you speak French?___
   B: ___No, I can't.___ (I can't speak French.)

3. A: Can gabrielle fix her printer?
   B: No, she can't (Gabrielle can't fix her printer.)

4. A: _____
   B: Yes, I can (I can whistle.)

5. A: Can carmen ride bike?
   B: No, she can't (Carmen can't ride a bike.)

6. A: Can
   B: Yes, It can (Elephants can swim.)

7. A: _____
   B: Yes, I can (The doctor can see you tomorrow.)

8. A: _____
   B: No, we can't (We can't have pets in the dorm.)

Work with a partner. Take turns asking and answering questions.
  Partner A: Ask a question. Begin with **Can you . . . ?**
  Partner B: Answer the question. Then ask **How about you?** and repeat the question.

Example: speak Arabic
PARTNER A: Can you speak Arabic?
PARTNER B: Yes, I can. OR No, I can't. How about you? Can you speak Arabic?
PARTNER A: Yes, I can. OR No, I can't. Your turn now.

PARTNER A	PARTNER B
1. ride a motorcycle	1. ride a horse
2. play the guitar	2. play the drums
3. float on water	3. whistle
4. touch your knee with your nose	4. touch your ear with your elbow
5. drive a stick-shift car	5. fix a flat tire
6. spell Mississippi	6. spell the teacher's last name

a stick shift

❏ **Exercise 11. Listening.** (Chart 12-3)

Listen to the conversations. Complete the sentences with the words you hear.

  1. A: Hello?

     B: _____ speak to Mr. Hudson, please?

     A: I'm sorry. _____ to the phone right now.

        _____ take a message? _____ return your call in about

        a half-hour.

     B: Yes. Please tell him Ron Myerson called.

2. A: _____ me lift this box?

    B: It looks very heavy. _____ to help you, but I think we need a third person.

    A: No, I'm pretty strong. I think _____ it together.

3. A: _____ the TV. _____ turn it up?

    B: _____ turn it up. I'm doing my homework.

    A: _____ your homework in another room?

    B: Oh, all right.

❏ **Exercise 12. Reading.** (Charts 12-1 → 12-3)
Read the paragraph. Complete the questions.

Color Blindness

    Some people can't see all the colors. They are color-blind. It doesn't mean they can't see any colors. But they have trouble seeing the difference between certain colors. They might confuse red and green or blue and purple. For example, people with red-green color blindness can't see the difference between the red light and the green light on a traffic light. But they can still drive safely because they can see the brightness of the lights. If the light is red, for example, it will also be bright. Look at the picture below. People with red-green color blindness can't see the number. Can you see the number?

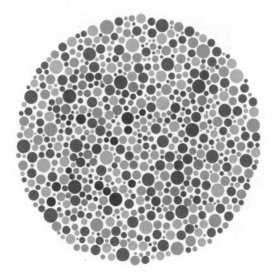

1. Color-blind people   can / can't   see all colors.

2. People who are color-blind   can / can't   drive.

3. If you can't see the number in the picture, you   are / aren't   color-blind.

❑ **Exercise 13. Warm-up.** (Chart 12-4)

Make sentences with some of the phrases from the box. Take turns completing the sentences with a partner.

Example:
PARTNER A: I (*can/can't*) fix a leaky faucet.
            Do you know how to fix a leaky faucet?
PARTNER B: Yes, I do. OR No, I don't.

a leaky faucet

> change the oil in a car   read musical notes
> ✓ fix a leaky faucet   solve algebra problems
> make ice cream   write computer code for an app★

12-4 Using *Know How To*

(a) I *can* swim.	Both *can* and *know how to* express ability.
(b) I *know how to swim*.	*Know how to* expresses something a person learned to do.
(c) *Can* you cook?	
(d) *Do* you *know how to cook*?	

❑ **Exercise 14. Let's talk: pairwork.** (Chart 12-4)

Work with a partner. Take turns asking and answering questions.

Do you know how to . . .

1. cook?
2. dance?
3. play soccer?
4. replace a zipper?
5. get to the airport from here?
6. fix a computer hard drive?
7. write with both your left and right hands?
8. wiggle your nose?
9. knit?
10. make a YouTube video?

★ *app* = an application; a small, special program for a smartphone or tablet

Exercise 15. Speaking and writing: pairwork. (Chart 12-4)

Part I. Work with a partner. Make questions about the people in the chart. Use **know how to**.

ABILITY	JERRY	ALEXA	BILL AND TINA	YOU
1. change the oil in a car	no	yes	yes	
2. start a fire without matches	yes	yes	no	
3. type without looking at the keyboard	no	no	yes	

Part II. Write three questions and answers about the people in the chart.

1. *Does Alexa know how to start a fire without matches? Yes, she does.*

2. _____

3. _____

Exercise 16. Let's write: small groups. (Chart 12-4)

Work in small groups. Complete the sentences together. Use a separate sheet of paper. Share some of your completions with the class.

1. Three-year-olds know how to _____.

2. Three-year-olds don't know how to _____.

3. Birds know how to _____.

4. Birds don't know how to _____.

5. We know how to _____.

6. We don't know how to _____.

7. (*name of a classmate*) knows how to _____.

8. Our teacher doesn't know how to _____.

9. Do you know how to _____?

Exercise 17. Warm-up. (Chart 12-4)

Choose the verb that is true for you.

Two years ago, I . . .

1. could / couldn't   speak English.

2. could / couldn't   drive a car.

3. could / couldn't   communicate with people from around the world.

12-5 Using *Could:* Past of *Can*

(a) Jake has a sore knee. He *can* walk, but he *can't* run.	*could* = the past form of *can*★
(b) Jake had a sore knee *last week*. He *could* walk, but he *couldn't* run.	NEGATIVE *could* + *not* = *couldn't*
(c) *Could you speak* English before you came here?	QUESTION *could* + *subject* + *main verb*

★Do not use the affirmative form of *could* for one completed action in the past.

    INCORRECT: *A week ago, Marc could pass his test.* One option is the simple past:

    CORRECT: *A week ago, Marc passed his test.* ***Be able to*** is also possible (see Chart 12-6).

❏ **Exercise 18. Let's talk: pairwork.** (Chart 12-5)

Work with a partner. Choose the answers that describe your childhood. Then tell your partner what you could and couldn't do when you were a child.

When I was a child, ...

1. I could stand on my head.	yes	no
2. I could sing in another language.	yes	no
3. I could tell time before the age of five.	yes	no
4. I could do cartwheels.	yes	no
5. I could read at the age of six.	yes	no
6. I could hold my breath underwater for one minute.	yes	no

a cartwheel

❏ **Exercise 19. Looking at grammar.** (Chart 12-5)

Complete the sentences by using *couldn't*. Use the expressions from the box or your own words.

call you	go to the movie
come to class	hear us
✓ finish my homework	light the candles
get into my car	wash his clothes
go swimming	watch TV

1. I ____couldn't finish my homework____ last night because I was too tired.

2. I _____ yesterday because I lost your
   telephone number.

3. I _____ last night because my TV is broken.

4. Theo _____ because he didn't have
   any matches.

5. The teacher _____ yesterday because he was sick.

6. My grandmother _____ at the party last night
   because her hearing aid was broken.

7. Nat _____ because he didn't have any
   laundry soap.

8. We _____ yesterday because the water was too cold.

9. I _____ yesterday because I locked all the
   doors and left the keys inside.

10. I _____ last night because I had to study.

❏ **Exercise 20. Let's talk: pairwork.** (Chart 12-5)
Work with a partner. Take turns making sentences with *because*.

SITUATION: Mr. Kostis had a bad day yesterday. There are many things he wanted to do
but couldn't. Tell what he couldn't do yesterday and give a reason.

Examples: eat breakfast \ get up late
    → Mr. Kostis couldn't eat breakfast because he got up late.

    go downtown during the day \ have to work
    → Mr. Kostis couldn't go downtown during the day because he had to work.

1. eat lunch \ leave his wallet at home
2. finish his report \ have to go to a meeting
3. leave work at five \ have to finish his report
4. play tennis after work \ it \ be raining
5. enjoy dinner \ his wife \ be angry at him
6. watch his favorite TV show after dinner \ his TV \ not work
7. read quietly \ his children \ be very noisy
8. go to bed early \ his neighbors \ come to visit

□ **Exercise 21. Let's talk: class activity.** (Chart 12-5)
Your teacher will make a statement. Give some of the negative results for the situations.
Use **can't** or **couldn't**. Close your book for this activity.

Example:
TEACHER (*book open*):   There was no heat in the classroom yesterday.
STUDENT (*book closed*): We couldn't stay warm.

1. I have only (*a small amount of money*) in my pocket / in my purse today.
2. Some people don't know how to use a computer.
3. Your parents had rules for you when you were a child.
4. This school has rules for students.
5. You didn't know much English last year.
6. You don't speak fluent English yet.
7. Millions of people in the world live in poverty.

□ **Exercise 22. Check your knowledge.** (Charts 12-1 → 12-5)
Correct the mistakes.

1. Could you ~~to~~ drive a car when you were sixteen years old?
2. If your brother goes to the graduation party, he can meets my sister.
3. I couldn't opened the door because I didn't have a key.
4. Tyler know how to use sign language. He learned it when he was a child.
5. Please turn up the radio. I can't to hear it.
6. Where we can meet for our study group?
7. You cannot to change your class schedule. The deadline was last week.
8. Are you knowing how to fix a leaky faucet?
9. When Ernesto arrived at the airport last Tuesday, he can't found a parking space.
10. Excuse me. You can help me? I'm looking for a pair of work boots.
11. Mr. Lo was born in Hong Kong, but now he lives in Canada. He cannot understand spoken English before he moved to Canada, but now he speak and understand English very well.

Exercise 23. Warm-up. (Chart 12-6)

Match each sentence on the left with its meaning on the right.

Column A

1. I can help you now.
2. I'm sorry I couldn't help you last night.
3. I can't help you tomorrow.
4. I can help you next week.
5. I can't help you now.

Column B

a. I wasn't able to help you.
b. I won't be able to help you.
c. I am able to help you.
d. I am not able to help you.
e. I will be able to help you.

12-6 Using *Be Able To*

PRESENT	(a) I *am able to touch* my toes. (b) I *can touch* my toes.	Examples (a) and (b) have basically the same meaning.
FUTURE	(c) I *will be able to go* shopping tomorrow. (d) I *can go* shopping tomorrow.	Examples (c) and (d) have basically the same meaning.
PAST	(e) I *wasn't able to finish* my homework last night. (f) I *couldn't finish* my homework last night.	Examples (e) and (f) have basically the same meaning.

Exercise 24. Looking at grammar. (Chart 12-6).

On a separate sheet of paper, make sentences with the same meaning as the given sentences. Use *be able to*.

1. I can be here tomorrow at ten o'clock.

   → *I'll (I will) be able to be here tomorrow at ten o'clock.*

2. Two students couldn't finish the test.

   → *Two students weren't able to finish the test.*

3. Kalil is bilingual. He can speak two languages.
4. Nola can get her own apartment next year.
5. Can you touch your toes without bending your knees?
6. Alec couldn't describe the thief.
7. I couldn't sleep last night because my apartment was too hot.
8. My roommate can speak four languages. He's multilingual.
9. I'm sorry that I couldn't call you last night.
10. I'm sorry, but I can't come to your party next week.
11. We're going to drive to San Francisco for our vacation. Can we do it in one day?

Exercise 25. Reading and grammar. (Chart 12-6)

Part I. Read the story.

Maya's English Experience

Five years ago, Maya moved to Canada with her young children. They couldn't speak English. Her children started school and learned English very quickly. Maya didn't study English and could just say basic, common sentences. She only understood people who spoke very slowly and used simple language.

Maya felt very frustrated. She heard about an evening English program at a local community center. She enrolled and began to study. At first, she couldn't understand or say very much. But slowly she got better. She was excited when she went shopping and could have short conversations with the cashier. Her kids were also excited. They could talk to her in English.

Today Maya's English is pretty good. She can talk to friends and neighbors. She watches TV and can understand a lot of it. Maya and her kids speak to each other in both English and their native language. She can switch back and forth very easily. Maya encourages friends to take classes. She says, "Don't worry. Try it for a few months. You can do it!"

Part II. Underline all the verbs with *could, couldn't,* and *can.* Rewrite the sentences using a form of *be able to*.

1. _____

2. _____

3. _____

4. _____

5. _____

6. _____

7. _____

8. _____

9. _____

Exercise 26. Listening. (Charts 12-1 → 12-6)

Listen to the conversations. Complete the sentences with the words you hear.

1. A: _____ to talk to Adam last night?

   B: _____ reach him. I _____ again later today.

2. A: _____ pizza?

   B: Yes, I _____ it. What about you?

   A: No, but _____ me?

   B: Sure.

3. A: _____ the teacher?

   B: I _____ her in the beginning, but now I

   _____ most of her lectures.

   A: I still _____ her very well.

4. A: Professor Castro, when _____ correct our tests?

   B: I began last night, but I _____ finish.

   I _____ again tonight. I hope _____

   hand them back to you tomorrow.

5. A: Hello?

   B: Hi. This is Jan Quinn. I'm wondering if _____ get in to see
   Dr. Novack today or tomorrow.

   A: Well, she _____ you tomorrow morning at 11:00.

   _____ in then?

   B: Yes, _____. Please tell me where you are. I _____ the
   way to your office.

❏ **Exercise 27. Warm-up.** (Chart 12-7)

Choose the correct response.

The weather is too warm.

a. I want to spend the day outside.
b. Let's turn on the air-conditioning.

12-7 Using *Very* and *Too* + Adjective

(a) The coffee is **very** hot, but I **can** drink it.	**Very** and **too** come in front of adjectives; *heavy* and *hot* are adjectives.
(b) The coffee is **too** hot. I **can't** drink it.	**Very** and **too** do NOT have the same meaning.
(c) The box is **very** heavy, but Tom **can** lift it.	In (c): *very heavy* = It is difficult but possible for Tom to lift the box.
(d) The box is **too** heavy. Bob **can't** lift it.	In (d): *too heavy* = It is impossible for Bob to lift the box.

Tom

Bob

(e) The coffee is **too** hot. NEGATIVE RESULT: I can't drink it.	In the speaker's mind, the use of **too** implies a negative result.
(f) The weather is **too** cold. NEGATIVE RESULT: We can't go to the beach.	

❏ **Exercise 28. Let's talk.** (Chart 12-7)
Make sentences for each picture. Use **very** or **too** and **can** or **can't** to describe the pictures.

Example: suitcase \ heavy \ lift
→ The suitcase is very heavy, but Mark can lift it.
→ The suitcase is too heavy. Benny can't lift it.

Mark

Benny

1. shoes \ tight \ wear

Marika

Mai

2. coat \ small \ wear

Bruno

Emily

3. soup \ hot \ eat

Salman

Ricardo

4. problem \ hard \ solve

Alan

Talal

Exercise 29. Looking at grammar. (Chart 12-7)
Complete the sentences with expressions from the box.

buy it	lift it
do his homework	reach the cookie jar
eat it	sleep
go camping	take a break

1. The soup is too hot. I can't _____

2. The diamond ring is too expensive. I can't _____

3. The weather is too cold. We can't _____

4. I am too busy. I can't _____

5. Samir is too tired. He can't _____

6. Peggy is too short. She can't _____

7. It's too noisy in the dorm at night. I can't _____

8. The couch is too heavy. I can't _____

❑ **Exercise 30. Looking at grammar.** (Chart 12-7)
Complete the sentences. Use *too* + adjectives from the box.

expensive	small	tired	windy
heavy	tall	uncomfortable	young

1. You can't lift a car. A car is _____

2. Jimmy is ten. He can't drive a car. He's _____

3. I can't sleep on an airplane. It's _____

4. I don't want to go fishing on the lake today. The weather is _____

5. Rachel doesn't want to play tennis this afternoon. She's _____

6. I can't buy a new car. A new car is _____

7. Patrick has gained weight. He can't wear his old shirt. It's _____

8. The basketball player can't stand up straight in the subway car. He's

   _____

❑ **Exercise 31. Looking at grammar.** (Chart 12-7)
Complete the sentences. Use *too* or *very*.

1. The tea is ____*very*____ hot, but I can drink it.

2. The tea is ____*too*____ hot. I can't drink it.

3. I can't put my wallet in my pocket. My pocket is _____ small.

4. An elephant is _____ big. A mouse is _____ small.

5. I can't buy a boat because it's _____ expensive.

6. A sports car is _____ expensive, but Daniella can buy one if she wants to.

7. We went to the Swiss Alps for our vacation. The mountains are _____
   beautiful.

8. I can't eat this food because it's _____ salty.

9. Larisa doesn't like her dorm room. She thinks it's _____ small.

10. I lost your jacket. I'm _____ sorry. I'll buy you a new one.

11. A: Do you like your math course?

    B: Yes. It's _____ difficult, but I enjoy it.

12. A: Do you like your math course?

    B: No. It's _____ difficult. I don't understand the problems.

13. A: Did you enjoy your dinner last night?

    B: Yes. The food was _____ good.

14. A: Are you going to buy that dress?

    B: No. It doesn't fit. It's _____ big.

15. A: My daughter wants to get married.

    B: What? But she can't! She's _____ young.

❑ **Exercise 32. Reading and listening.** (Chapter 12)

Part I. Read the story. Look at new vocabulary with your teacher first.

Memory Champions

Nelson Dellis is a memory champion. He can remember a lot of information. For example, he can look at a page of 500 numbers and say all of them. He can go through a deck of cards and say each number with its suit (diamonds, spades, hearts, and clubs) — in order.

> **Do you know these words?**
>
> champion
> a deck of cards
> suit (in a deck of cards)
> amazing
> train

Dellis won the 2011 U.S.A. Memory Championship. He was able to memorize 248 numbers in five minutes. He was also able to memorize a complete deck of cards in 63 seconds.

Memory champions can do amazing things. After they look at photos of 100 strangers, the memory champions can memorize the first and last names with the correct spelling in 15 minutes!

Dellis can't remember all this information naturally. He needs to study. He trains every day. One way he remembers names is to create pictures in his mind. For example, if Dellis wants to remember a person's last name, like "Hardy," he can imagine something "hard," like wood. Then he connects this picture to the person's face. Maybe he sees wood on top of the person's head. When he sees the face again, it will help him remember the name "Hardy."

Memory champions say they aren't special. They believe that with years of practice a person can develop a great memory.

Part II. Complete the sentences with ideas from the reading.

1. Nelson Dellis is a memory champion because he _____

2. In 2011, Dellis was able to memorize _____

3. When memory champions see photos of 100 strangers, they can _____

   _____

4. Dellis can do amazing things with his memory, but he can't _____

   _____

5. With a lot of training and practice, people _____

Part III. Complete the sentences with the words you hear.

1. Dellis _____ remember long rows of numbers.

2. Dellis _____ memorize a complete deck of cards.

3. In 2011, Dellis _____ win the U.S.A. Memory Championship.

4. Dellis _____ remember all this information naturally.

5. Memory champions _____ make pictures in their minds.

6. They say that with a lot of work a person _____ have a good memory.

❏ **Exercise 33. Check your knowledge.** (Chapter 12)
Correct the mistakes.

1. We ~~will~~ can go to the museum tomorrow afternoon.

2. Can you to memorize a deck of cards?

3. I saw a beautiful diamond necklace at a store yesterday, but I couldn't bought it.

4. The shirt is too small. I can wear it.

5. Sam Garder know how to count to 1,000 in English.

6. When I was on vacation, I can swim every day.

7. Honeybees not able to live in very cold climates.

8. Where we can go in the city for a good meal?

9. Hiroshi can reads in five languages.

10. I'm late. I'm too sorry. I didn't be able to find a parking spot.

❑ **Exercise 34. Writing.** (Chapter 12)

Part I. First, read the writing sample. Then think about a character (person, animal, or creature) from fiction. This character can do amazing things. Write a paragraph about this character. (If you can't think of a character, create your own and give it a name.)

Superman

    Superman can do amazing things. He can fly very fast. He is able to jump over tall buildings. He has X-ray vision, so he can see through objects like buildings. He is very strong. He can bend steel, and he is able to lift cars and trains.

    But there is one thing he can't do. He can't be around kryptonite. Kryptonite is a metal, and it makes Superman very weak. He isn't able to use his special powers. When Superman is away from kryptonite, he becomes strong again.

    I admire Superman. He uses his powers in good ways. He fights for truth and justice. He catches criminals and rescues people in trouble. He is a hero.

Superhero

Include this information in your paragraph:

- Begin with this sentence: _____ *can do amazing things*.
- Give examples of things the character can do. Use *can* and *be able to*.
- Is there anything the character can't do? Give examples.
- Explain why he or she likes to do these things.
- Finish with this sentence: *I admire/don't admire* _____. Give reasons.

Part II. Editing check: Work individually or change papers with a partner. Check (✓) for the following:

1. _____ indented paragraph

2. _____ capital letter at the beginning of each sentence

3. _____ period at the end of each sentence

4. _____ no *to* with *can* or *can't*

5. _____ use of *too* for a negative result

6. _____ correct use of *is* + *able to* and *are* + *able to*

7. _____ correct spelling (use a dictionary or computer spell-check)

Chapter 13

Modals, Part 2: Advice, Necessity, Requests, Suggestions

❑ **Exercise 1. Warm-up.** (Chart 13-1)
Read about Ella's problem. Choose all the sentences that you agree with.

Ella bought a pair of shoes. After a week, the heel on one of her shoes broke. She was at work and didn't have another pair of shoes to wear. She had to miss a meeting with clients because she couldn't walk in a broken shoe.

She should . . .

1. take the shoes back to the store and get her money back.
2. take the shoes back to the store and get another pair of the same shoes.
3. fix the heel with glue.
4. write a letter to the store owner and ask for money because she missed a meeting.
5. never buy shoes with high heels again.
6. use social media to warn people about these shoes.

13-1 Using *Should*

(a) My clothes are dirty. I **should wash** them. (b) Tom is sleepy. He **should go** to bed. (c) You're sick. You **should see** a doctor.	**Should** means "This is a good idea. This is good advice."
(d) I You She He } **should go.** It We They	**Should** is followed by the base form of a verb. INCORRECT: *He should goes.* INCORRECT: *He should to go.*
(e) You **should not leave** your grammar book at home. You need it in class. (f) You **shouldn't leave** your grammar book at home.	NEGATIVE: *should not* CONTRACTION: *should + not = shouldn't*

❑ **Exercise 2. Looking at grammar.** (Chart 13-1)
Complete the conversations. Begin each sentence with *You should*. Use the expressions from the box or your own words.

call the credit card company	put on a bandaid
call the manager	see a dentist
drink tea with honey	sew it
find an ATM	study harder
✓ go to the post office	take a nap

1. A: I want to mail a package.

   B: _____You should go to the post office._____

2. A: I'm sleepy.

   B: _____

3. A: I need to get some cash.

   B: _____

4. A: I have a toothache. I think I have a cavity.

   B: _____

5. A: I'm getting bad grades in all of my classes at school.

   B: _____

6. A: The toilet in my apartment doesn't work.

   B: _____

7. A: I lost my credit card.

   B: _____

8. A: My shirt has a hole under the arm.

   B: _____

9. I have a blister on my big toe. You should _____

10. My voice is hoarse. You should _____

❑ **Exercise 3. Let's talk: small groups.** (Chart 13-1)

Work in small groups. Make sentences with **should** and **shouldn't**. Share some of your answers with the class.

SITUATION 1: Dina has a headache from working at her computer too long.

Dina . . .

   a. see a doctor.

   b. take some medicine for her headache.

   c. lie down.

   d. go to the hospital emergency room.

   e. take a 15-minute break from the computer.

SITUATION 2: Nick stayed late after school to help his teacher. He missed the last bus and needs a ride home. It takes two hours to walk to his home, and it is a 15-minute ride by car.

Nick . . .

   a. call a taxi.

   b. hitchhike.

   c. ask his teacher for a ride.

   d. call a friend for a ride.

   e. walk.

SITUATION 3: Lydia's baby doesn't want to take a nap. He is crying.

Lydia . . .

   a. hold him.

   b. rock him.

   c. let him cry until he falls asleep.

   d. feed him.

   e. let him play.

SITUATION 4: The teacher is giving a final exam. One student keeps looking at a paper under his exam paper. It has the answers on it.

The teacher . . .

   a. take the paper away and give the student another chance.

   b. give the student a failing grade for the test.

   c. give the student a failing grade for the class.

   d. send the student to see the director of the school.

SITUATION 5: Marisa is 16 years old. A boy in her class wants her to go to dinner and a movie with him. This will be her first date.

Her parents . . .

   a. let her go if her older brother goes too.   d. let her go by herself.

   b. tell her to wait until she is older.   e. let her go to dinner only.

   c. go with her.

❏ **Exercise 4. Looking at grammar.** (Chart 13-1)
Complete the sentences with *should* or *shouldn't*.

1. Students _____*should*_____ come to class every day.

2. Students _____*shouldn't*_____ skip class.

3. We _____ waste our money on things we don't need.

4. It's raining. You _____ take your umbrella when you leave.

5. Timmy, you _____ pull the cat's tail!

6. People _____ hurt animals.

7. Your plane leaves at 8:00 A.M. You _____ get to the airport
   by 6:00.

8. Life is short. We _____ waste it.

9. You _____ smoke because it's bad for your health.

10. When you go to New York City, you _____ see a play on Broadway.

11. You _____ walk alone on city streets after dark. It's dangerous.

12. We _____ cross a street at an intersection. We
    _____ jaywalk.

❏ **Exercise 5. Let's talk: small groups.** (Chart 13-1)
Work in small groups. Each person presents a situation. The group gives advice by making a list of sentences using *should* and *shouldn't*.

SITUATION 1: English is not my native language. What advice can you give me about good ways to learn English?

SITUATION 2: I am a teenager. What advice can you give me about how to live a healthy lifestyle?

SITUATION 3: I am a newcomer. What advice can you give me about this school and this city?

SITUATION 4: I have a job interview tomorrow. What advice can you give me about going to a job interview?

SITUATION 5: I have a lot of trouble sleeping. I often wake up in the middle of the night and can't go back to sleep. What advice can you give me to help me sleep better?

❏ **Exercise 6. Listening.** (Chart 13-1)
Listen to each sentence and choose the verb you hear. After you check your answers, listen again. If you agree, circle *yes*. If you don't agree, circle *no*.

			DO YOU AGREE?	
1.	should	shouldn't	yes	no
2.	should	shouldn't	yes	no
3.	should	shouldn't	yes	no
4.	should	shouldn't	yes	no
5.	should	shouldn't	yes	no
6.	should	shouldn't	yes	no
7.	should	shouldn't	yes	no
8.	should	shouldn't	yes	no

❏ **Exercise 7. Warm-up.** (Chart 13-2)
Which two sentences have the same meaning?

1. I want to spell-check my writing.
2. I need to spell-check my writing.
3. I have to spell-check my writing.
4. I should spell-check my writing.

13-2 Using *Have* + Infinitive (*Have To / Has To / Had To*)

(a) People *need to eat* food. (b) People *have to eat* food.	Examples (a) and (b) have basically the same meaning.
(c) Jack *needs to study* for his test. (d) Jack *has to study* for his test.	Examples (c) and (d) have basically the same meaning. ***Have*** + *infinitive* has a special meaning: it expresses the same idea as ***need***.
(e) I *had to study* last night.	PAST FORM: ***had*** + *infinitive*
(f) *Do* you *have to* leave now? (g) What time *does* Jim *have to* leave? (h) Why *did* they *have to* leave yesterday?	QUESTION FORM: ***do***, ***does***, or ***did*** is used in questions with ***have to***.
(i) I *don't have to* study tonight. (j) The concert was free. We *didn't have to* buy tickets.	NEGATIVE FORM: ***don't***, ***doesn't***, or ***didn't*** is used with ***have to***.

❏ **Exercise 8. Looking at grammar.** (Chart 13-3)
Rewrite the sentences using the correct form of ***have to***.

1. I need to cash a check. _____ *I have to cash a check.* _____

2. Ellen needs to get a haircut. _____

3. The kids need to eat lunch. _____

4. The kids needed to eat lunch. _____

5. Jason needs to leave now. _____

6. Does Petra need to leave right now? _____

7. Why did you need to sell your car? _____

8. Malia doesn't need to work late. _____

9. The employees didn't need to work late. _____

10. The restaurant needed to close early. _____

❏ **Exercise 9. Let's talk: class activity.** (Chart 13-2)
Answer the questions your teacher asks you. Close your book for this activity.

1. What do you want to do today?
2. What do you have to do today?
3. What do you want to do tomorrow?
4. What do you have to do tomorrow?

5. What does a student need to do or have to do?

6. Who has to go shopping? Why?

7. Who has to go to the post office? Why?

8. Who has to go to the bank? Why?

9. Where do you have to go today? Why?

10. Where do you want to go tomorrow? Why?

11. What did you have to do yesterday? Why?

12. Did you have responsibilities at home when you were a child? What did you have to do?

13. If you're driving a car and the traffic light turns red, what do you have to do?

14. What do you have to do before you cross a busy street?

15. Do you have to learn English? Why?

16. Who has a job? What are some of the things you have to do when you're at work?

17. What kind of job did you have in the past? What did you have to do when you had that job?

❏ **Exercise 10. Let's talk: class activity.** (Chart 13-2)
Make sentences using *have to*/*has to* and *because*.

Example: go to the mall / buy some new shoes
STUDENT A: I have to go to the mall because I have to buy some new shoes.
   TEACHER: (*to Student B*) Why does (*Student A*) have to go to the mall?
STUDENT B: (*Student A*) has to go to the mall because he/she has to buy some new shoes.

1. go to the drugstore / buy some toothpaste

2. go to the grocery store / get some flour and sugar

3. go shopping / get a new coat

4. go to the post office / pick up a package

5. stay home tonight / study grammar

6. go to the hospital / visit a friend

7. go to the bank / cash a check

8. go downtown / go to the immigration office

9. go to the bookstore / buy a notebook

10. go to (*name of a store in the city*) / buy (*a particular thing at that store*)

❏ **Exercise 11. Looking at grammar.** (Chart 13-2)
Complete the sentences with the words in parentheses. Use a form of *have*/*has* + *infinitive*.

1. A: Franco can't join us for dinner tonight. (*he, work*) ___He has to work.___

   B: (*he, work*) ___Does he have to work___ tomorrow night too? If he doesn't,

   maybe we should postpone dinner until then.

2. A: Why (*you, go*) _____ to the library tonight?

    B: (*I, find*) _____ some information for my research paper.

3. A: Patricia's flight is at eight tonight. What time (*she, leave*) _____
    _____ for the airport?

    B: Around five. (*she, be*) _____ there a little early to meet
    her group.

4. A: Why did you go to the bookstore after class yesterday?

    B: (*I, buy*) _____ some colored pencils.

    A: Oh? Why (*you, buy*) _____ colored pencils?

    B: I need them for some drawings I plan to do for my art class.

5. A: (*I, go*) _____ to the store.

    B: Why?

    A: Because (*I, get*) _____ some rice and fresh fruit.

6. A: Katie didn't come to the movie with us last night.

    B: Why?

    A: Because (*she, study*) _____ for a test.

7. A: What time (*you, be*) _____ at the dentist's office?

    B: Three. I have a three o'clock appointment.

8. A: (*Ted, find*) _____ a new apartment?

    B: Yes, he does. His old apartment is too small.

9. A: (*Miki, take, not*) _____ another English course.
    Her English is very good.

    B: (*you, take*) _____ another English course?

    A: Yes, I do. I need to study more English for my job.

10. A: Was Vince at home yesterday evening?

    B: No. (*he, stay*) _____ late at the office.

    A: Why?

    B: (*he, finish*) _____ a report for his boss.

❑ Exercise 12. Listening. (Chart 13-2)

In spoken English, ***have to*** is often pronounced "hafta." ***Has to*** is often pronounced "hasta." Listen to each sentence and choose the correct verb.

Example: You will hear: We have to go now.
You will choose: (have to)   has to

1. have to	has to		6. have to	has to
2. have to	has to		7. have to	has to
3. have to	has to		8. have to	has to
4. have to	has to		9. have to	has to
5. have to	has to		10. have to	has to

❑ Exercise 13. Warm-up. (Chart 13-3)

Match each sentence to the correct meaning.

At the gym

1. Children under 12 must have
   an adult with them. ____

2. Children under 12 should have
   an adult with them. ____

3. Children under 12 have to have
   an adult with them. ____

a. It's a good idea.

b. There is no choice.

13-3 Using *Must, Have To / Has To*, and *Should*

MUST vs. HAVE TO

(a) People need food. People *have to eat* food. (b) People need food. People *must eat* food.	Examples (a) and (b) have basically the same meaning: *must eat = have to eat* **Have to** is more common in spoken English. **Must** is more common in written instructions and rules. Adults also use **must** with children. It is very strong.
(c) I You She He } *must work*. It We They	**Must** is followed by the base form of a verb. INCORRECT: *He must works.* INCORRECT: *He must to work.*

NEGATIVE: MUST vs. HAVE TO

(d) You *must not text* while you are driving. (e) You *don't have to go* to the movie with us if you don't want to.	**must not** = Don't do this! You don't have a choice.
	don't have to = It's not necessary; you have a choice.

MUST vs. SHOULD

MUST	*SHOULD*
Something is very important. Something is necessary. You do not have a choice.	Something is a good idea, but you have a choice.
(f) You *must take* an English course. You cannot graduate without it. (g) Johnny, look at me. You *must eat* your vegetables. You can't leave the table until you eat your vegetables.	(h) You *should take* an English course. It will help you. (i) Johnny, you *should eat* your vegetables. They're good for you. You'll grow up to be strong and healthy.

❑ **Exercise 14. Let's talk: small groups.** (Chart 13-3)
Work in small groups. Make two additional rules for each item.

1. Rules about driving/traffic:
   a. You must stop at a red light.
   b. You must not text and drive.

   c. _____

   d. _____

2. Rules on an airplane:
   a. You must fasten your seat belt during takeoff and landing.
   b. You must not smoke.

   c. _____

   d. _____

3. Rules a parent gives a young child:
   a. You must not run into the street.
   b. You must sit in a car seat in the car.

   c. _____

   d. _____

❏ **Exercise 15. Looking at grammar.** (Chart 13-3)
Complete the sentences. Use ***must*** and expressions from the box.

apply in person	pay income tax
✓ have a driver's license	pay the first and last month's rent
have a medical license	put on a jacket
have a passport	take one tablet every six hours

1. According to the law,* a driver _____ *must have a driver's license.* _____

2. Mansour wants to get a job. According to the application, he _____

   _____ at 500 Broadway Avenue.

3. I want to travel abroad. According to the law, I _____

4. If you want to be a doctor, you _____

5. Davey! It's cold outside. You _____

6. Arthur's doctor gave him a prescription. According to the directions on

   the bottle, Arthur _____

7. I want to rent an apartment. According to the rental agreement, I

   _____

8. Pia has a job in Chicago. She earns a good salary. According to the law,

   she _____

---

*according to the law = the law says

❏ **Exercise 16. Looking at grammar.** (Charts 13-2 and 13-3)
Choose the correct completion.

1. If you want to keep your job, you ____ be late for work.

   a. must not   b. don't have to   c. doesn't have to

2. My office is near my apartment, so I can walk to work. I ____ take a bus. I take a bus only in bad weather.

   a. must not   b. don't have to   c. doesn't have to

3. Some schools require their students to wear uniforms to school, but my children's school doesn't require uniforms. They ____ wear uniforms to school.

   a. must not   b. don't have to   c. doesn't have to

4. Billy, it is very important to be careful with matches. You ____ play with matches.

   a. must not   b. don't have to   c. doesn't have to

5. Kevin is twenty-four, but he still lives with his parents. That saves him a lot of money. For example, he ____ pay rent or buy his own food.

   a. must not   b. don't have to   c. doesn't have to

6. Carly, the water in that river is polluted. You ____ play in it.

   a. must not   b. don't have to   c. doesn't have to

7. If you have a credit card, you ____ pay for things in cash. You can charge them.

   a. must not   b. don't have to   c. doesn't have to

8. Kyra is going to buy school supplies. She has a coupon for 20% off, so she ____ pay full price.

   a. must not   b. don't have to   c. doesn't have to

9. When an airplane is taking off, you have to be in your seat with your seat belt on. You ____ stand up and walk around when an airplane is taking off.

   a. must not   b. don't have to   c. doesn't have to

10. When Mrs. Wilson drives to the supermarket, she ____ park far away because she has a disabled person's parking permit for her car.

    a. must not   b. don't have to   c. doesn't have to

Exercise 17. Let's talk: small groups. (Charts 13-1 → 13-3)

Work in small groups. Make sentences about your English class. Use **should** / **have to** / **don't have to** with the given phrases. Share a few of your answers with the class.

Example: Students . . . study.
Response: Students have to study.

Students . . .

1. come to class.
2. sit quietly.
3. take attendance.
4. bring a pencil and some paper to class.
5. listen carefully.
6. speak English in class.
7. stand up when the teacher enters the room.
8. knock on the door before entering the room.
9. raise their hands when they want to talk.
10. do their homework.
11. memorize vocabulary.
12. bring an English–English dictionary to class.
13. write homework answers in their books.

Exercise 18. Listening. (Charts 13-1 and 13-3)

Listen to each pair of sentences. One sentence uses **should**, and the other uses **must**. Decide which sentence you agree with. Discuss your answers as a class.

Example: You will hear: a. People must learn how to use computers.
                       b. People should learn how to use computers.

You will choose: *a OR b*

1. _____   4. _____   7. _____

2. _____   5. _____   8. _____

3. _____   6. _____   9. _____

Exercise 19. Warm-up. (Chart 13-4)

Which two questions are more polite?

Child to parent

1. May I have a snack?
2. Can I have a snack?
3. Could I have a snack?

13-4 Polite Questions: *May I*, *Could I*, and *Can I*

(a) *May I borrow* your pen? (b) *Could I borrow* your pen? (c) *Can I borrow* your pen?	Examples (a), (b), and (c) have the same meaning: I want to borrow your pen. I am asking politely to borrow your pen. *Could* is more polite and formal than *can*. *May* is very polite and formal.
(d) *May I please borrow* your pen? (e) Could I *please* borrow your pen? (f) Can I *please* borrow your pen?	*Please* makes the request more polite.
TYPICAL RESPONSES (g) *Yes, of course.* (h) *Of course.* (i) *Certainly.* (j) *Sure.* (informal)* (k) *No problem.* (informal)	TYPICAL CONVERSATION A: *May I please borrow your pen?* B: *Yes, of course.* *Here it is.* A: *Thank you.* / *Thanks.*

*Informal English is typically used between friends and family members.

❑ **Exercise 20. Let's talk: pairwork.** (Chart 13-4)

Work with a partner. Look at the pictures. Write conversations. Use *May I*, *Can I*, or *Could I* and typical responses.

1

2

3

4

❏ **Exercise 21. Let's talk: pairwork.** (Chart 13-4)
Work with a partner. Ask and answer polite questions using *May I*, *Can I*, or *Could I*.

Example: Your partner has a pencil. You want to borrow it.
PARTNER A: May I (please) borrow your pencil?
PARTNER B: Sure. Here it is.
PARTNER A: Thank you. Your turn now.

PARTNER A	PARTNER B
1. Your partner has a calculator. You want to borrow it.	1. Your partner has some notebook paper. You forgot your notebook, and you need one piece of paper.
2. Your partner has an eraser. You want to use it for a minute.	2. Your partner has a pencil sharpener. You want to borrow it.
3. You are at your partner's home. You want to use the bathroom.	3. You are at your partner's home. You want a glass of water.
4. You are at a restaurant. Your partner is a server. You want to have a cup of coffee.	4. You are at a restaurant. Your partner is a server. You want to leave, and you need the check.*

❏ **Exercise 22. Warm-up.** (Chart 13-5)
Do the sentences have the same or a different meaning?

1. Could you hold the elevator for me?
2. Would you hold the elevator for me?

13-5 Polite Questions: *Could You* and *Would You*

(a) ***Could you*** (*please*) ***open*** the door? (b) ***Would you*** (*please*) ***open*** the door?	Examples (a) and (b) have the same meaning: I want you to open the door. I am asking you politely to open the door.
TYPICAL RESPONSES (c) *Yes, of course.* (d) *Certainly.* (e) *I'd be glad to.* (f) *I'd be happy to.* (g) *Sure.* (informal) (h) *No problem.* (informal)	A TYPICAL CONVERSATION A: *Could you please open the door?* B: *I'd be glad to.* A: *Thank you. / Thanks.*

*the check = the bill in a restaurant

Work with a partner to complete the conversations. Use *Could you* or *Would you* and give typical responses. Then write them down and discuss them with the rest of the class.

1. A: Excuse me, sir. _____

   B: _____

   A: _____

2. A: _____

   B: Excuse me? I didn't understand you.

   A: _____

   B: _____

❑ **Exercise 24. Let's talk: pairwork.** (Chart 13-5)

Work with a partner. Make requests and give answers. Use *Could you* or *Would you*.

Example: You want your partner to open the window.
PARTNER A: Could you (please) open the window?
PARTNER B: Sure.
PARTNER A: Thank you.

You want your partner to . . .

1. close the door.
2. turn on the light.
3. turn off the light.
4. pass you the salt and pepper.

5. hand you that book.
6. translate a word for you.
7. tell you the time.
8. hold your books for a minute.

❏ **Exercise 25. Let's talk: pairwork.** (Chart 13-5)

Work with a partner. Ask and answer polite questions that fit each situation. Share your conversations with the rest of the class.

Example: A professor's office: Partner A is a student. Partner B is the professor.
PARTNER A: (*knocks on door*) May I come in?
PARTNER B: Certainly. Come in. How are you today?
PARTNER A: Fine, thanks. Could I talk to you for a few minutes? I have some questions about the last assignment.
PARTNER B: Of course. Have a seat.
PARTNER A: Thank you.

1. A restaurant: Partner A is a customer. Partner B is a server.
2. A classroom: Partner A is a teacher. Partner B is a student.
3. A kitchen: Partner A is a parent. Partner B is a teenager.
4. A clothing store: Partner A is a customer. Partner B is a salesperson.
5. An apartment: Partner A and B are roommates.
6. A car: Partner A is a passenger. Partner B is the driver.
7. An office: Partner A is a manager. Partner B is an employee.
8. A house: Partner B answers the phone. Partner A wants to talk to (*someone*).

❏ **Exercise 26. Warm-up.** (Chart 13-6)

What do you think is a good suggestion for each situation? Use ***Run!*** or ***Don't run!*** Discuss your answers with the class.

a bear

a cougar

13-6 Imperative Sentences

(a) A: **Close the door,** Jimmy. It's cold outside. B: Okay, Mom.	In (a): **Close the door** is an IMPERATIVE SENTENCE. The sentence means "Jimmy, I want you to close the door. I am telling you to close the door."
(b) **Sit** down. (c) **Be** careful!	An imperative sentence uses the base form of a verb (*close, sit, be, etc.*). The subject is **you**. Sit down. = (You) sit down.
(d) **Don't open** the window. (e) **Don't be** late.	NEGATIVE IMPERATIVE **don't** + the base form of a verb
(f) ORDERS: **Stop,** thief! (g) DIRECTIONS: **Open** your books to page 24. (h) ADVICE: **Don't worry.** (i) REQUESTS: **Please close** the door.	Imperative sentences give orders, commands, directions, and advice. With the addition of **please,** as in (i), imperatives sound more polite.

❑ **Exercise 27. Let's talk.** (Chart 13-6)
Write the correct command for each picture.

> Don't let go!   Hurry up!   March!   Relax.   Wait for me!

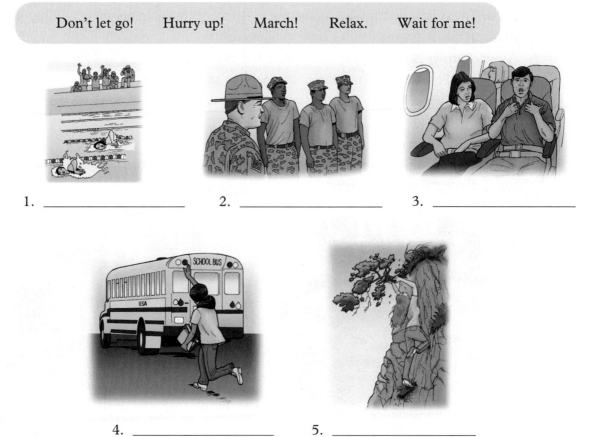

1. _____   2. _____   3. _____

4. _____   5. _____

❏ **Exercise 28. Looking at grammar.** (Chart 13-6)

Underline the imperative verbs in the conversations.

1. TOM: What's the matter?

   JIM: I have the hiccups.

   TOM: Hold your breath.

   BOB: Drink some water.

   JOE: Breathe into a paper bag.

   KEN: Eat a piece of bread.

   JIM: It's okay. My hiccups are gone.

2. ANYA: I need to leave now.

   IVAN: Wait for me.

   ANYA: Don't forget your keys.

   IVAN: I have them.

3. ANDY: Bye, Mom. I'm going over to Billy's house.

   MOM: Wait a minute. Did you clean up your room?

   ANDY: I'll do it later.

   MOM: No. Do it now, before you leave.

   ANDY: What do I have to do?

   MOM: Hang up your clothes. Make your bed. Put your books back on the shelf.
   Empty the wastepaper basket. Okay?

   ANDY: Okay.

❏ **Exercise 29. Looking at grammar.** (Chart 13-6)

Look at the pictures. Write an imperative sentence for each one.

1. _____   2. _____

3. _____   4. _____

❏ **Exercise 30. Reading and writing.** (Chart 13-6)

Part I. Read the conversation. Look at new vocabulary with your teacher first.

QUESTION: How do I get to the post office from here?
DIRECTIONS: Walk two blocks to 16th Avenue. Then turn
right on Forest Street. Go two more blocks to Market Street
and turn left at the light. The post office is halfway down the
street on the right-hand side.

Do you know these words?

block
turn right/left
halfway
right-hand

Part II. Complete this question: How do I get to ____ from
here? Then write directions. Use four or more imperative
verbs. Here is some vocabulary you may want to use.

walk	right-hand side	up the street
turn right	left-hand side	down the street
go (to)	cross	in the middle of the street
turn left	crosswalk	at the light

❏ **Exercise 31. Let's talk: class activity.** (Chart 13-6)

Listen to your teacher's questions. Make some imperative sentences for these situations.
Close your book for this activity.

Example:
TEACHER: Your friend has a headache. What are some typical suggestions?
STUDENT A: Take an aspirin.
STUDENT B: Lie down and close your eyes for a little while.
STUDENT C: Put a cold cloth on your forehead.
STUDENT D: Don't read for a while.
STUDENT E: Take a hot bath and relax.
            Etc.

1. You are the teacher of this class. You are assigning homework for tomorrow. What
   are some typical imperative sentences for this situation?

2. Your friend is coughing and sneezing. What are some typical imperative sentences for
   this situation?

3. Your eight-year-old son/daughter is walking out the door to go to school. What are
   some typical imperative sentences for this situation?

4. Your friend is going to cook rice for the first time this evening. Tell him/her how to
   cook rice.

5. Your friend wants to win a scholarship to a university. Tell him/her what to do and what not to do.

6. A friend from another country is going to visit your country for the first time next month. Tell him/her what to do and what to see as a tourist in your country.

❏ **Exercise 32. Warm-up.** (Chart 13-7)
Complete each sentence with all the possible verbs from the box.

can	has	is able	is going	may

1. Nate _____ to come the meeting.

2. Petra _____ come to the meeting.

13-7 Modal Auxiliaries

(a) Anita { can / could / may / might / must / should / will } go to class.		An auxiliary is a helping verb. It comes in front of the base form of a main verb. The following helping verbs are called "modal auxiliaries": **can, could, may, might, must, should, will, would**.
(b) Anita { is able to / is going to / has to } go to class.		Expressions that are similar to modal auxiliaries are **be able to, be going to, have to**.

❏ **Exercise 33. Looking at grammar.** (Chart 13-7)
Add **to** where necessary. If **to** is not necessary, write **Ø**.

1. My sister can ____Ø____ play the guitar very well.

2. We have ____to____ pay our rent on the first of the month.

3. Could you please _____ open the window? Thanks.

4. I wasn't able _____ visit my friends yesterday because I was busy.

5. You shouldn't _____ drink twenty cups of coffee a day.

6. Will you _____ be at the meeting tomorrow?

7. Does everyone have _____ be at the meeting?

8. You must not _____ miss the meeting. It's important.

9. Vanessa might not _____ be there tomorrow.

10. May I _____ use your phone?

11. We couldn't _____ go to the concert last night because we didn't have tickets.

12. Can you _____ play a musical instrument?

13. What time is the plane going _____ arrive?

14. It may _____ be too cold for us to go swimming tomorrow.

13-8 Summary Chart: Modal Auxiliaries and Similar Expressions

AUXILIARY*	MEANING	EXAMPLE
(a) *can*	ability	I *can* sing.
	polite question	*Can* you please help me?
(b) *could*	past ability	I *couldn't* go to class yesterday.
	polite question	*Could* you please help me?
(c) *may*	possibility	It *may* rain tomorrow.
	polite question	*May* I help you?
(d) *might*	possibility	It *might* rain tomorrow.
(e) *must*	necessity	You *must* have a passport.
(f) *should*	advisability	You *should* see a doctor.
(g) *will*	future event	My sister *will* meet us at the airport.
(h) *would*	polite question	*Would* you please open the door?
(i) *be able to*	ability	I *wasn't able to* attend the meeting.
(j) *be going to*	future event	Tina *is going to* meet us at the airport.
(k) *have to/has to*	necessity	I *have to* study tonight.
(l) *had to*	past necessity	I *had to* study last night too.

*See the following charts for more information: *can*, Chart 12-1, p. 361, and Chart 12-3, p. 365; *could*, Chart 12-5, p. 370; *may* and *might*, Chart 11-1, p. 334; *must*, Chart 13-3, p. 392; *should*, Chart 13-1, p. 383; *will*, Chart 10-6, p. 319, Chart 10-7, p. 321, and Chart 11-1, p. 334; *would*, Chart 13-5, p. 397; *be able to*, Chart 12-6, p. 373; *be going to*, Chart 10-1, p. 303; *have/has/had to*, Chart 13-2, p. 388.

❑ **Exercise 34. Let's talk: small groups.** (Chart 13-8)
Work in small groups. Each person in the group should give a different response. Share a few of your answers with the class.

Example: Name something you *had to* do yesterday.
STUDENT A: I had to go to class.
STUDENT B: I had to go to the post office to buy some stamps.
STUDENT C: I had to study for a test.

1. Name something you *can* do.

2. Name something you *couldn't* do yesterday.

3. Name something you *may* do tomorrow.

4. Name something you *might* do tomorrow.

5. Name something you *must* do this week.

6. Name something you *have to* do today.

7. Name something you *don't have to* do today.

8. Name something you *should* do this evening.

9. Name something you *will* do this evening.

10. Name something you *are going to* do this week.

11. Name something you *weren't able to* do when you were a child.

12. Name something you *had to* do when you were a child.

13. You want to borrow something from a classmate. Ask a polite question with *could*.

14. You want a classmate to do something for you. Ask a polite question with *would*.

15. A classmate has something that you want. Ask a polite question with *may*.

16. Name something that *may* happen in the world in the next ten years.

17. Name something that (probably) *won't* happen in the world in the next ten years.

18. Name some things that this school *should* do to make it a better place for students.

❑ **Exercise 35. Looking at grammar.** (Chart 13-8)
Choose the correct completion.

1. Doug _____ every day.
   a. shaves   b. is shaving   c. has to shaves

2. _____ to class every day?
   a. Are you go   b. Do you have to go   c. You going

3. Matsu _____ to be here tomorrow.
   a. might   b. is going   c. must

4. Carl _____ be in class yesterday.
   a. didn't   b. wasn't   c. couldn't

5. Fatima _____ to her sister on the phone yesterday.
   a. spoke   b. can speak   c. speaks

6. I _____ my rent last month.
   a. might pay   b. will pay   c. paid

7. I want to go to a movie tonight, but I _____ home and study.
   a. should stay   b. stayed   c. stay

8. We _____ downtown tomorrow.
   a. going   b. might go   c. will can go

9. _____ you like some hot coffee now?
   a. Will   b. Would   c. Do

❏ **Exercise 36. Listening.** (Chart 13-8)

Listen to each sentence. Choose the sentence that is closest in meaning.

Example: You will hear: It might snow tomorrow.
            You will choose: a. It will snow.   (b.) It may snow.   c. It must snow.

1. a. Tom should work.
   b. Tom must work.
   c. Tom might work.

2. a. Becky can swim.
   b. Becky may swim.
   c. Becky will swim.

3. a. The teacher should correct papers.
   b. The teacher had to correct papers.
   c. The teacher wanted to correct papers.

4. a. You may study for the test.
   b. You must study for the test.
   c. You should study for the test.

5. a. We should go to a movie.
   b. It's possible we will go to a movie.
   c. We have to go to a movie.

6. a. We couldn't help.
   b. We didn't need to help.
   c. We weren't able to help.

7. a. I didn't want to go to school.
   b. I didn't have to go to school.
   c. I wasn't able to go to school.

Part I. Read the article. Look at new vocabulary with your teacher first.

packaging

a receipt

Returning an Item to a Store

Many stores have a return policy* for items you buy. Generally, you must have a receipt for a return. Some stores may have your purchase on their computer, but most require a receipt.

Do you know these words?

item
purchase
exception
exchange
unpleasant

In general, clothes must still have the tags. Stores don't want you to wear something and then return it. Usually, you can wear shoes, but you have to stay on carpets and not walk outside in them. The soles of the shoes should look like new. It is also important to keep the box and other packaging. Stores would like to resell the item, so they want to have the original packaging.

There is usually a time limit for returns. Some stores might give you two weeks, while others may give you 90 days. A few stores have no time limit because they want you to be completely satisfied.

If you buy electronics, like a computer or a TV, there is often a restocking fee. This is a charge to put the item back on the shelf. Often the fee is 15 percent of the cost or more. Here's an example. John bought a camera, but he couldn't understand how to use it. He decided to return it. The company returned his money but kept 15 percent of the camera cost. There is an exception. If an item is defective (damaged or broken), the company will probably return all your money. Generally, a DVD or CD is not returnable if you open it. Be sure you are going to keep it before you open the packaging.

---

* *return policy* = rules a store has for returning an item

Items on sale usually have this policy: "All sales final." This means there are no returns on sale items. Sometimes a store might let you exchange the item for something else.

Every store is different, so it is important to ask about the return policy before you buy. Simply say, "What is your return policy for ____?" You may save yourself some unpleasant surprises if you get all the information before you buy.

Part II. Complete the sentences with the correct verb according to the article.

1. In general, you ____ have a receipt if you want to return something.
   a. might   b. must

2. The store ____ have information about your purchase on its computer.
   a. might   b. will

3. If you want to return shoes, you ____ wear them outside.
   a. don't have to   b. must not

4. Generally, you ____ keep the original packaging if you want to return an item.
   a. must   b. may

5. A store ____ give you two weeks to return an item.
   a. must   b. may

6. If you buy an item and it is broken, you ____ return it.
   a. can   b. can't

7. At most stores, you ____ return sale items.
   a. can   b. can't

8. You ____ ask the salesperson about the store's return policy.
   a. should   b. will

❏ **Exercise 38. Warm-up.** (Chart 13-9)
Imagine you are Speaker B. What answers do you like?

A: It's a beautiful day.

B: a. Let's watch TV.

   b. Let's go to the beach.

   c. Let's go to the park.

   d. Let's go hiking.

   e. Let's play video games.

13-9 Using *Let's*

(a) A: What should we do tonight?
   B: **Let's go to a movie.**
   A: Okay.
 	
(b) A: I'm tired.
   B: I'm tired too. **Let's take a break.**
   A: That's a good idea!
	Let's (*do something*) = I have a suggestion for you and me. *Let's* = Let us
	
	In (a): *Let's go to a movie.* = I think we should go to a movie. Do you want to go to a movie?

❏ **Exercise 39. Looking at grammar.** (Chart 13-9)
Complete the conversations with **let's**. Use the words from the box or your own words.

eat get a cup of coffee go dancing go to Florida go to a movie	go to a seafood restaurant go swimming ✓ leave at six-thirty just stay home and relax walk

1. A: What time should we leave for the airport?

   B: _____Let's leave at six-thirty._____

   A: Okay.

2. A: Where should we go for our vacation?

   B: _____

   A: That's a good idea.

3. A: Where do you want to go for dinner tonight?

   B: _____

4. A: The weather is beautiful today. _____

   B: Okay. Great!

5. A: I'm bored. _____

   B: I can't. I have to study.

6. A: Should we take the bus downtown or walk downtown?

   B: It's a nice day. _____

7. A: Dinner's ready. The food's on the table.

   B: Great! _____. I'm starving.

8. A: Where should we go Saturday night?

   B: _____

   A: Wonderful idea!

9. A: We have an hour between classes. _____

   B: Okay. That sounds good.

❏ **Exercise 40. Let's talk: pairwork.** (Chart 13-9)
Work with a partner. Take turns making suggestions with *let's*. Give two suggestions for each situation.

Example: It's a beautiful day today. What should we do?
PARTNER A: It's a beautiful day today. What should we do?
PARTNER B: Let's go to Woodland Park Zoo.
PARTNER A: That's a possibility. Or, let's go to the beach.

1. I don't have to work tonight. What should we do?
2. Next Monday's a holiday and there's no school. We should do something fun.
3. I don't know anyone at this party. I want to leave.
4. What time should we leave for the airport tomorrow? There will be a lot of traffic.
5. It's your birthday next week. What would you like to do?
6. Parent to child: I have a little free time right now. I can spend it with you.

❏ **Exercise 41. Check your knowledge.** (Chapters 12 and 13)
Correct the mistakes.

1. Would you please to help me?

2. I will can go to the meeting tomorrow.

3. My brother wasn't able calling me last night.

4. Tariq should calls us.

5. I have to went to the store yesterday.

6. Susie! You must not to hit your brother!

7. May you please hand me that book?

8. Alessandra couldn't answered my question.

9. Shelley can't goes to the concert tomorrow.

10. Let's going to a movie tonight.

11. Don't to interrupt. It's not polite.

12. Can you to stand on your head?

13. I saw a beautiful dress at a store yesterday, but I couldn't bought it.

14. Closing the door, please. Thank you.

15. May I please to borrow your dictionary? Thank you.

❏ **Exercise 42. Reading and writing.** (Chapter 13)
Part I. Read the passage about Manhattan. Look at new vocabulary with your teacher.

A Great Place to Visit

capital letter →

I grew up in Manhattan.* Manhattan is a very exciting part of New York City. You should go there because there are so many interesting sights to see.

> **Do you know these words?**
> incredible
> landmark

First, the museums are amazing. You can find art, natural science, and history museums. My favorite museum is on Ellis Island. Ellis Island was the entry point for immigrants from 1892 to 1954, and you can learn a lot about history. My family came through Ellis Island, and I was able to find my grandparents' names.

Many tall buildings have incredible views of the city. You can go to the top of the Empire State Building, Rockefeller Center, or even the Statue of Liberty. Take your camera because you will want to get great photos. The most popular places have long lines, so you should check wait times before you go. Sometimes you have to make reservations.

Statue of Liberty

---

* See Appendix Chart A5-1, p. 487 for capitalization rules for place names.

A good way to learn about the city is to take a boat tour. Manhattan is an island, and you can see many famous landmarks from the water. A tour guide can tell you a lot about the history of the sites and the different neighborhoods. It's also fun to ride under the famous bridges, like the Brooklyn Bridge.

Central Park is very beautiful and relaxing. It's a wonderful place for walking, running, biking, boating, or just people-watching. Sometimes there are concerts in the park. Millions of people visit the park every year, but it's very large, so it doesn't feel crowded.

There is something else you should know. Manhattan is very expensive. Make sure you have enough money and be careful when you are walking around town. Keep your money in a safe place and stay away from dangerous places. Your hotel can tell you about places you shouldn't visit.

If you go to Manhattan, you will have special memories. Don't forget to send me pictures!

Part II. Write a paragraph about your hometown or a city you like. Imagine you are talking to someone who wants to visit your hometown (or choose another city). First, answer these questions:

- Why is your hometown (or other city) a good place for me to visit?
- What should I do when I'm there?
- Where should I go?
- What should I see?
- Are there places I shouldn't visit?

Begin this way:

I grew up in _____. It is a very exciting/beautiful/interesting place. You should go there because there are so many wonderful sights to see. OR

One of my favorite places to visit is _____. It is a very exciting/beautiful/interesting city, and there are many wonderful sights to see.

Part III. Editing check: Work individually or change papers with a partner. Check (✓) for the following:

1. _____ indented paragraph

2. _____ capital letter at the beginning of each sentence

3. _____ capital letter for cities and place names (See Appendix Chart A5-1, p. 487.)

4. _____ period at the end of each sentence

5. _____ use of some modal verbs

6. _____ correct spelling (use a dictionary or computer spell-check)

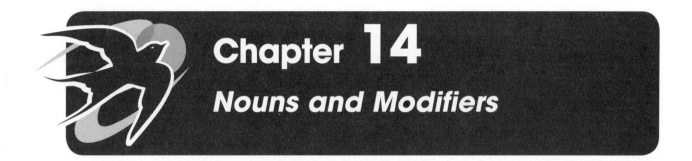

Chapter 14
Nouns and Modifiers

❏ **Exercise 1. Warm-up.** (Chart 14-1)
Match the sentences to the pictures. Are the words in red used as nouns or adjectives?

1. an old computer
2. a computer mouse
3. a computer keyboard

Picture A

Picture B

Picture C

14-1 Modifying Nouns with Adjectives and Nouns

ADJECTIVE + NOUN (a) I bought an **expensive** *book*. (b) I bought **expensive** *books*.	Adjectives can modify nouns, as in (a) and (b). See Chart 6-3, p. 164, for a list of common adjectives. NOTE: Adjectives do not have plural forms. *INCORRECT: expensives books*
NOUN + NOUN (c) I bought a *grammar* *book*. (d) I bought *grammar* *books*.	Nouns can modify other nouns. In (c) and (d): *grammar* is a noun that is used as an adjective to modify another noun (*book/books*).
NOUN + NOUN (e) He works at a **shoe** *store*. *INCORRECT: He works at a shoes store.*	A noun that is used as an adjective is usually in the singular form. In (e): the store sells shoes, but it is called a **shoe** (singular form) **store**.
ADJECTIVE + NOUN + NOUN (f) I bought an **expensive** *grammar* *book*. *INCORRECT: I bought a grammar expensive book.*	Both an adjective and a noun can modify a noun, as in (f); the adjective comes first, the noun second.

❏ **Exercise 2. Looking at grammar.** (Chart 14-1)
Underline each adjective and draw an arrow to the noun it modifies. اﻟﺧط ﺗﺣت ﻧﺿﻊ adj

وﯾﻌدﻣﺎ ﻧﺿﻊ ﺳﮭم ﻋﻠﻰ اﻟﻣﻛﺎﯾب

1. I drank some <u>hot</u> tea.

2. My grandmother is a smart woman.

3. English is not my native language.

4. The busy waitress poured coffee into the empty cup.

5. A young man carried the heavy suitcase for his pregnant wife.

6. I slept in an uncomfortable bed at an old hotel.

❏ **Exercise 3. Looking at grammar.** (Chart 14-1)
Underline each noun used as an adjective and draw an arrow to the noun it modifies.

1. We sat at the <u>kitchen</u> table.

2. Have you paid the phone bill yet?

3. We met Steve at the train station.

4. Vegetable soup is nutritious.

5. The movie theater is next to the furniture store.

6. The waiter handed us a lunch menu.

7. The traffic light was red, so we stopped.

8. Ms. Bell gave me her business card.

❏ **Exercise 4. Listening.** (Chart 14-1)
Listen to the sentences. Decide if the given word is used as a noun or adjective.

Example: You will hear: This **grammar** book has a lot of information.
You will choose: NOUN   (ADJ)

1. kitchen	NOUN	ADJ	6. car	NOUN	ADJ	
2. kitchen	NOUN	ADJ	7. car	NOUN	ADJ	
3. apartment	NOUN	ADJ	8. chicken	NOUN	ADJ	
4. apartment	NOUN	ADJ	9. chicken	NOUN	ADJ	
5. music	NOUN	ADJ	10. grammar	NOUN	ADJ	

□ **Exercise 5. Let's talk: small groups.** (Chart 14-1)

Work in small groups. Which noun in the box can be used with all three of the nouns used as modifiers? For example, in the first sentence, the completion can be *a university education, a high school education,* or *a college education.*

class   number   race   store
✓education   official   room   tickets
keys   program   soup   trip

1. Regina has a ⎰university ⎱ _____education._____
                ⎱high school⎰
                  college

2. We went to a ⎰furniture⎱ _____Store_____
                ⎱shoe   ⎰
                 clothing

3. I took a ⎰history⎱ _____class_____
            ⎱math   ⎰
             science

4. We watched a ⎰horse⎱ _____race_____
                ⎱car ⎰
                 foot

5. I talked to a ⎰government⎱ _____official._____
                 ⎱city   ⎰
                  school

6. Mom made some ⎰vegetable⎱ _____soup_____
                 ⎱bean   ⎰
                  chicken

7. He told me about a ⎰radio   ⎱ _____Program_____
                      ⎱computer⎰
                       TV

8. We took a/an ⎰boat   ⎱ _____trip_____
                ⎱bus   ⎰
                 airplane

9. We visited Meg in her ⎰hospital⎱ _____room_____
                         ⎱hotel   ⎰
                          dorm

10. We bought some ⎰theater⎱ _____tickets_____
                   ⎱concert⎰
                    airplane

11. I couldn't find my { car / house / locker } ___Keys_____

lockers   license plate

12. What is your { phone / apartment / license plate } ___number_____

❏ **Exercise 6. Looking at grammar.** (Chart 14-1)

Complete the sentences. Use the information in the first part of the sentence. Use a noun that modifies another noun in the completion.

1. Vases for flowers are called ___*flower vases*_____.

2. A cup for coffee is called a ___*coffee cup*_____.

3. An article in a newspaper is called a _News Paper article___.

4. Rooms in hotels are called _hotels rooms_____.

5. A worker in an office is called an _Office worker_____.

6. A tag that gives the price of something is called a _Price tag_____.

7. Seats on airplanes are called _airplanes Seats_____.

8. A bench in a park is called a _Park bench_____.

9. Soup that is made of beans is called _____.

10. A house that is made of bricks is called a _____.

Exercise 7. Looking at grammar. (Chart 14-1)

Each item lists two nouns and one adjective. Write them in the correct order.

n   1. homework   The teacher gave us a ___*long homework assignment*___.
adj long
n   assignment

2. show   I watched a __good TV show__.
   good
   TV

3. road   We drove on a _____.
   mountain
   dangerous

4. car   Sofia was in a __bad car accident__.
   bad
   accident

5. ₃ article   I read an _____.
   ₂ magazine
   ₁ interesting

6. ₁ delicious   Mrs. Montero made some _____.
   ₂ vegetable
   ₃ soup

7. ₂ card   My sister gave me a _____.
   ₁ funny
   ₃ birthday

8. ₁ narrow   People don't like to sit in _____.
   ₂ seats
   ₃ airplane

❏ **Exercise 8. Warm-up.** (Chart 14-2)

Answer the questions. Then complete the description.

1. Is it large?   yes   no

2. Is it expensive?   yes   no

3. What is the stone? _____

Now describe it: a _____ _____ _____ ring.
                        a. size   b. cost   c. material

14-2 Word Order of Adjectives

(a) a *large red* car *INCORRECT: a red large car*	In (a): two adjectives (*large* and *red*) modify a noun (*car*). Adjectives follow a particular order. In (a): an adjective describing SIZE (*large*) comes before an adjective describing COLOR (*red*).
(b) a *beautiful young* woman (c) a *beautiful red* car (d) a *beautiful Greek* island	The adjective **beautiful** expresses an opinion. Opinion adjectives usually come before all other adjectives. In (b): opinion precedes age. In (c): opinion precedes color. In (d): opinion precedes nationality.
(e) **OPINION ADJECTIVES** dangerous favorite important difficult good interesting dirty happy strong expensive honest wonderful	There are many opinion adjectives. The words in (e) are examples of common opinion adjectives.

USUAL WORD ORDER OF ADJECTIVES					
(1)	(2)	(3)	(4)	(5)	(6)
OPINION	**SIZE**	**AGE**	**COLOR**	**NATIONALITY***	**MATERIAL**
beautiful	large	young	red	Greek	metal
delicious	tall	old	blue	Chinese	glass
kind	little	middle-aged	black	Mexican	plastic

(f) some *delicious Mexican* food (g) a *small glass* vase (h) a *kind old Chinese* man	A noun is usually modified by only one or two adjectives, although sometimes there are three.
(i) RARE a *beautiful small old brown Greek metal* coin	It is very rare to find a long list of adjectives in front of a noun.

* NOTE: Adjectives that describe nationality are capitalized: *Korean, Venezuelan, Saudi Arabian, etc.*

☐ **Exercise 9. Looking at grammar.** (Chart 14-2)
Describe each picture. Use two or three adjectives for each noun. Answers may vary.

Example:

OPINION	SIZE	AGE	COLOR	NATIONALITY	MATERIAL	NOUN
expensive	Ø	Ø	*gray*	Ø	*wool*	*suit*

1

OPINION	SIZE	AGE	COLOR	NATIONALITY	MATERIAL	NOUN

2

OPINION	SIZE	AGE	COLOR	NATIONALITY	MATERIAL	NOUN

3

OPINION	SIZE	AGE	COLOR	NATIONALITY	MATERIAL	NOUN

4

OPINION	SIZE	AGE	COLOR	NATIONALITY	MATERIAL	NOUN

5

Made in France

100% silk

OPINION	SIZE	AGE	COLOR	NATIONALITY	MATERIAL	NOUN

❏ **Exercise 10. Looking at grammar.** (Chart 14-2)
Complete each sentence with a word from the box.

Asian	✓cotton	designer
brick	important	soft
Canadian	glass	unhappy

1. Marcos is wearing a white _____*cotton*_____ shirt.

2. Hong Kong is an important _____ city.

3. Luke likes to wear expensive _____ suits.

4. Misha was a/an _____ little boy when he broke his favorite toy.

5. Teresa has a/an _____ wool blanket on her bed.

6. Our dorm is a tall red _____ building.

7. The laptop computer is a/an _____ modern invention.

8. I keep leftover food in round _____ containers.

9. Ice hockey is a popular _____ sport.

❏ **Exercise 11. Looking at grammar.** (Chart 14-2)
Put the given words in the correct order.

1. red   a _____*big red*_____ tomato
   big

2. delicious some _____ food
   Thai

3. red   some _____ tomatoes
   small

4. old   some _____ cows
   big
   brown

5. narrow   a _____ road
   dirt

6. young   a _____ woman
   serious

7. long   _____ hair
   black
   beautiful

8. Chinese   a/an _____ work of art
   famous
   old

9. leather   a _____ belt
   brown
   thin

10. wonderful   a/an _____ story
    old
    Native American

□ **Exercise 12. Looking at grammar.** (Chart 14-2)
Add adjectives or nouns used as adjectives to complete the sentences. Share some of your answers with the class.

1. We had some hot _____ food.

2. My dog, Buddy, is a/an _____ old dog.

3. We bought a blue _____ blanket.

4. Alison has _____ gold earrings.

5. Jeremy has short _____ hair.

6. Mr. Yu is a/an _____ young man.

7. Omar lives in a large _____ brick house.

8. I bought a big _____ suitcase.

9. Sally picked a/an _____ red flower.

10. Charlie wore an old _____ shirt to the picnic.

❏ **Exercise 13. Looking at grammar.** (Charts 14-1 and 14-2)
Choose the correct completion.

1. Mr. Lane wore ____.
   a. a cotton shirt old   b. an old cotton shirt

2. She put some honey in a ____.
   a. blue glass jar   b. glass blue jar

3. The Great Wall is a ____.
   a. famous Chinese landmark   b. Chinese landmark famous

4. Len is a/an ____.
   a. man young honest   b. honest young man

5. Pizza is my ____.
   a. favorite food Italian   b. favorite Italian food

6. Vincent usually wears ____.
   a. brown old comfortable leather shoes   b. comfortable old brown leather shoes

7. I used a ____ to mail a gift to my sister.
   a. brown cardboard box   b. box brown cardboard

8. Ilya is a ____.
   a. handsome middle-aged man   b. middle-aged handsome man

❏ **Exercise 14. Let's talk: pairwork.** (Charts 14-1 and 14-2)
Work with a partner. Take turns giving a prompt and completing it with a noun.
Note: Don't let your intonation drop when you give the prompt.

Example: a dark . . .
PARTNER A: a dark . . .
PARTNER B: night (room, building, day, cloud, etc.)

1. a kitchen . . .
2. a busy . . .
3. a public . . .
4. a true . . .
5. some expensive . . .

Change roles.
6. a birthday . . .
7. a computer . . .
8. a baby . . .
9. a soft . . .
10. an easy . . .

Change roles.
11. a telephone . . .
12. a fast . . .
13. some comfortable . . .
14. a foreign . . .
15. a famous Italian . . .

Change roles.
16. an interesting old . . .
17. an airplane . . .
18. a dangerous . . .
19. a beautiful Korean . . .
20. some delicious Mexican . . .

Change roles.

21. a government . . .

22. some hot . . .

23. a flower . . .

24. a bright . . .

25. some small round . . .

Change roles.

26. a bus . . .

27. a history . . .

28. an icy cold . . .

29. a hospital . . .

30. a movie . . .

❑ **Exercise 15. Listening.** (Charts 14-1 and 14-2)

Listen to each sentence. Choose the best completion(s). There may be more than one answer.

Example: You will hear: We watched an interesting TV . . .
You will choose: a. store. (b.) movie. (c.) show.

1. a. card.   b. cake.   c. party.

2. a. friend.   b. bus.   c. keys.

3. a. jeans.   b. shoes.   c. flowers.

4. a. test.   b. classroom.   c. eraser.

5. a. room.   b. games.   c. desk.

6. a. mail.   b. article.   c. story.

❑ **Exercise 16. Game.** (Charts 14-1 and 14-2)

Work in teams. Your teacher will put 10–15 objects on a tray. You will have one minute to look at the tray. Then your teacher will take it away. Write down all the objects on the tray. Add adjectives to describe the objects. You will get one point for each object and one point for each adjective you use. The team with the most points wins.

❑ **Exercise 17. Warm-up.** (Chart 14-3)

Complete the sentences with words from the box. Give your opinion.

| good | bad | sweet | sour |

1. Lemons are _____.

2. Chocolate tastes _____.

3. Flowers smell _____.

14-3 Linking Verbs + Adjectives

(a) The flowers *were* *beautiful*. *BE* + ADJECTIVE		Adjectives can follow *be*, as in (a). The adjective describes the subject of the sentence. See Chart 1-7, p. 16.
LINKING VERB + ADJECTIVE (b) The flowers *looked* *beautiful*. (c) The flowers *smelled* *good*. (d) I *feel* *good*. (e) Candy *tastes* *sweet*. (f) That book *sounds* *interesting*.		Adjectives can follow a few other verbs. These verbs are called "linking verbs." The adjective describes the subject of the sentence. Common linking verbs are *look, smell, feel, taste,* and *sound*.

❑ **Exercise 18. Let's talk: pairwork.** (Chart 14-3)
Work with a partner. Take turns completing the sentences with linking verbs.

Part I. Make three sentences to tell your partner how you feel today. Begin each sentence with *I feel . . . .* Take turns using these words.

1. good
2. fine
3. terrible

4. lazy
5. nervous
6. happy

7. terrific
8. sleepy
9. tired

10. calm
11. sick
12. old

Part II. Take turns naming things that you can taste and smell.

13. taste good
14. taste terrible
15. taste delicious
16. taste sweet

17. taste sour
18. smell good
19. smell bad
20. smell wonderful

Part III. Take turns naming things that are . . .

21. clean.
22. dirty.

23. new.
24. old.

25. expensive.
26. comfortable.

27. uncomfortable.
28. messy.

❑ **Exercise 19. Let's talk.** (Chart 14-3)
Work in groups or as a class. Take turns showing and describing emotions.
  Student A: Choose one of the emotions listed below. Show that emotion with an expression on your face or with actions. Don't say the emotion you are trying to show.
  Student B: Describe how Student A looks. Use the linking verb *look* and an adjective.

1. angry
2. sad/unhappy

3. happy
4. tired/sleepy

5. busy
6. comfortable

7. surprised
8. nervous

Exercise 20. Looking at grammar. (Chart 14-3)
Use any possible completions for these sentences. Use the adjectives from the box or your own adjectives.

easy	delicious	terrible / awful
good / terrific / wonderful / great	interesting	tired / sleepy

1. Gabriela told me about a new book. I want to read it. It sounds _____*interesting /*_____
   _____*good / terrific / etc.*_____

2. Karen learned how to make paper flowers. She told me how to do it. It sounds
   _____*easy*_____.

3. There's a new comedy on TV tonight. I read a review of it and would like to watch it.
   It sounds _*wonderful*_____.

4. Professor Wilson is going to lecture on Internet security tomorrow evening. I think I'll
   go. It sounds _*inter*_____.

5. Chris explained how to fix a flat tire. I think I can do it. It sounds _____.

6. Marcia didn't finish her dinner because it didn't taste _____.

7. I put too much salt in the soup. Sorry, it tastes _____.

8. Amy didn't get any sleep last night because she studied all night for a final exam.
   Today she looks _____.

9. Yum! This dessert tastes _____. What is it?

10. A: What's the matter? Do you feel okay?
    B: No. I feel _____. I think I'm getting a cold.

11. A: Do you like my new dress, darling?
    B: You look _____, honey.

12. A: Pyew!* Something smells _____! Do you smell it too?
    B: I sure do. It's the garbage in the alley.

---

* Pyew is sometimes said "p.u." Both Pyew and p.u. mean that something smells very bad.

❑ **Exercise 21. Let's talk.** (Chart 14-3)

Work in pairs or small groups. Your teacher will choose a noun and give you a time limit (e.g., one minute, three minutes, etc.). Think of as many adjectives or nouns used as adjectives as you can that describe the given nouns. Make a list. Then your teacher will choose another noun.

Example: car

Response: big, little, fast, slow, comfortable, small, large, old, new, used, noisy, quiet, foreign, electric, antique, police, etc.

1. weather   3. food   5. country   7. river
2. animal   4. movie   6. person   8. student

❑ **Exercise 22. Warm-up.** (Chart 14-4)

Complete the sentences with the correct form of the word in red.

Example: Professor Hakim is a slow speaker. Professor Hakim speaks slowly.

Example: Martha is a careful writer. Martha writes carefully.

1. Pierre is a fluent Spanish speaker. He speaks Spanish _____.

2. Suzanne is a quick learner. She learns _____.

14-4 Adjectives and Adverbs

	ADJECTIVE	ADVERB	

(a) Ann is a *careful* driver.
        (adjective)
 	
(b) Ann drives *carefully*.
        (adverb)
	careful
	slow
	quick
	easy
		carefully
		slowly
		quickly
		easily
			An ADJECTIVE describes a noun.
			In (a): *careful* describes *driver*.
			
			An ADVERB describes the action of a verb.
			In (b): *carefully* describes *drives*.
			Most adverbs are formed by adding **-ly** to an adjective.

(c) John is a *fast* driver.
        (adjective)
 	
(d) John drives *fast*.
        (adverb)
	fast
	hard
	early
	late
		fast
		hard
		early
		late
			The adjective form and the adverb form are the same for *fast*, *hard*, *early*, and *late*.

(e) Linda is a *good* writer.
        (adjective)
 	
(f) Linda writes *well*.
        (adverb)
	good	**well**	***Well*** is the adverb form of ***good***.*

* *Well* can also be used as an adjective to mean "not sick." *Paul was sick last week, but now he's well.*

❑ **Exercise 23. Looking at grammar.** (Chart 14-4)
Choose the correct completion.

1. My hometown is small and   quiet / quietly.

2. Mr. Callis whispered. He spoke   quiet / quietly.

3. Anna pronounces every word   careful / carefully.

4. Samuel is a   careful / carefully   writer.

5. We like to go boating in   clear / clearly   weather.

6. Nathan has poor eyesight. He can't see   clear / clearly
   without his glasses.

7. Boris makes a lot of mistakes when he writes. He's a   careless / carelessly   writer.

8. Boris writes   careless / carelessly.

9. The teacher asked an   easy / easily   question.

10. I answered the teacher's question   easy / easily.

11. Fernando is kind, generous, and thoughtful. He is a   good / well   person.

12. Diana and I went to high school together. I know her   good / well.

❏ **Exercise 24. Looking at grammar.** (Chart 14-4)

Part I. Write adverb forms.

ADJECTIVE	ADVERB		ADJECTIVE	ADVERB
1. fast	_____		5. beautiful	_____
2. late	_____		6. fluent	_____
3. good	_____		7. hard	_____
4. easy	_____		8. early	_____

Part II. Write the correct adjective or adverb form. Use words from *Part I*.

1. Did you have a ____*good*____ sleep? Did you sleep _____?

2. The teacher speaks too _____. The students want her to slow down.

3. It rained _____ yesterday.

4. I forgot about my telephone bill. I paid it _____.

5. Do you want to be a _____ speaker of English?

6. Vincent lifted the heavy box _____. He's very strong.

7. Nadia speaks French _____. She has no accent.

8. Thank you! The flowers look _____.

❏ **Exercise 25. Looking at grammar.** (Chart 14-4)

Complete each sentence with the correct form (adjective or adverb) of the given words.

1. careful   Do you drive ____*carefully*____?

2. correct   Shari gave the _____ answer to the question.

3. correct   She answered the question _____.

4. fast   Justin is a _____ reader.

5. quick   Justin reads _____.

6. fast   Justin reads _____.

7. neat   Barbara has _____ handwriting. It is easy to read what she writes.

8. neat   Barbara writes _____.

9. hard   I study _____.

10. hard   The students took a _____ test.

11. honest   Roberto answered the question _____.

12. slow   Valery and Fumiko walked through the park _____.

13. quick   We were in a hurry, so we ate lunch _____.

14. careless   I made some _____ mistakes in my last composition.

15. early   Last night, we had dinner _____ because we had to
               leave for a meeting at 6:00.

16. early   We had an _____ dinner last night.

17. loud   I speak _____ when I talk to my grandfather
               because he has trouble hearing.

18. slow, clear Nina speaks English _____ and _____.

❑ **Exercise 26. Reading, grammar, and speaking.** (Charts 14-3 and 14-4)
Read the story. Put one line under each adjective. Put two lines under each adverb. Then
answer the questions in small groups.

Elvis Presley

Elvis Presley is very important to popular music. He
has a special title: the King of Rock and Roll. But when he
came on stage in the 1950s, he wasn't popular with many
parents. His style of dancing shocked them. They thought he
jumped around the stage too excitedly and danced wildly. His
music was a combination of country music and rhythm and

Do you know these words?

popular
shock
wild
combination
scream
appear
huge

blues. To many parents, he sang too loudly. They believed his music was bad for children. But audiences loved him and screamed for more. He kept making music, and he appeared on TV and in movies. Soon Elvis was a huge star.

1. Who is a popular singer right now?
2. Describe his/her type of music. Use several adjectives.
3. Why is he/she popular?

❑ **Exercise 27. Warm-up.** (Chart 14-5)
Which statement best describes the picture?

1. Some of the flowers are red.
2. All of the flowers are red.
3. Most of the flowers are red.

14-5 Expressions of Quantity: *All Of, Most Of, Some Of, Almost All Of*

(a) Rita ate **all of** *the food* on her plate.	**All of**, **most of**, and **some of** express quantities.
(b) Mike ate **most of** *his food*.	*all of* = 100%
(c) Susie ate **some of** *her food*.	*most of* = a large part but not all
	some of = a small or medium part
	NOTE: These expressions require a determiner (*the, his, her*, etc.).
	INCORRECT: *Most of food*
(d) Matt ate **almost all of** *his food*.	*all of* = 100%
INCORRECT: *Matt ate almost of his food*.	*almost all of* = close to 100%
	Almost is used with **all**, as in (d). **All** cannot be omitted.

❏ **Exercise 28. Looking at grammar.** (Chart 14-5)

Complete each sentence with (*almost*) *all of, most of,* or *some of*.

1. 2, 4, 6, 8: _____*All of*_____ these numbers are even.

2. 1, 3, 5, 7: _____ these numbers are odd.

3. 1, 3, 4, 6, 7, 9: _____ these numbers are odd.

4. 1, 3, 4, 6, 7, 8: _____ these numbers are odd.

5. 1, 3, 4, 5, 7, 9: _____ these numbers are odd.

6. _____ the birds in Picture A are flying.

7. _____ the birds in Picture B are flying.

8. _____ the birds in Picture C are flying.

9. _____ the birds in Picture D are flying.

Picture A

Picture B

Picture C

Picture D

10. _____ the students in this class have dark hair.

11. _____ the students in this class are using pens rather than pencils to do this exercise.

12. _____ the students in this class wear glasses.

13. _____ the students in this class can speak English.

❑ **Exercise 29. Warm-up.** (Chart 14-6)
Look at the phrases in red. <u>Underline</u> the noun and the quantity word. Decide which word the verb agrees with.

1. All of the money is in my wallet.
2. All of the coins are on the kitchen counter.

14-6 Expressions of Quantity: Subject–Verb Agreement

(a) *All of my* **work is** finished. (b) *All of my* **friends are** kind. (c) *Some of my* **homework is** finished. (d) *Some of my* **friends are** coming to my birthday party.	In (a): *all of* + **singular** noun + **singular** verb In (b): *all of* + **plural** noun + **plural** verb In (c): *some of* + **singular** noun + **singular** verb In (d): *some of* + **plural** noun + **plural** verb
	When a subject includes an expression of quantity, the verb agrees with the noun that immediately follows **of**.

COMMON EXPRESSIONS OF QUANTITY

all of	a lot of	most of
almost all of	half of	some of

❑ **Exercise 30. Looking at grammar.** (Chart 14-6)
Choose the correct completion.

1. All of that money _____*is*_____ mine.
   is/are

2. All of the windows _____ open.
   is/are

3. We saw one movie. Some of the movie _____ interesting.
   was/were

4. We saw five movies. Some of the movies _____ interesting.
   was/were

5. A lot of those words _____ new to me.
   is/are

6. A lot of that vocabulary _____ new to me.
   is/are

7. Half of the glasses _____ empty, and half of the glasses _____ full.
   _____is/are_____   _____is/are_____

8. Half of the glass _____ empty.
   _____is/are_____

IT'S HALF EMPTY.   IT'S HALF FULL.

Pessimist   Optimist

9. Almost all of the air in the city _____ polluted.
   _____is/are_____

10. Almost all of the rivers in this area _____ polluted.
    _____is/are_____

11. Most of the students _____ to class on time.
    _____comes/come_____

12. Most of our mail _____ in the morning.
    _____comes/come_____

❑ **Exercise 31. Listening.** (Charts 14-5 and 14-6)

Listen to each sentence. Circle the percentage that means the same as the quantity you hear.

Example: You will hear: Half of the coffee was gone.
            You will choose: 100% (50%) 10%

1. 100%   80%   10%
2. 100%   30%   0%
3. 90%   100%   10%
4. 10%   20%   70%
5. 25%   50%   85%

❑ **Exercise 32. Let's talk: class activity.** (Charts 14-5 and 14-6)

Your teacher will ask you questions. Answer each question using a complete sentence and an expression of quantity (*all of, most of, some of, a lot of, three of,* etc.). If the answer is zero, use *none of.* Close your book for this activity.

Example:
TEACHER: How many of the people in this room are wearing shoes?
STUDENT A: All of the people in this room are wearing shoes.
TEACHER: How many of us are wearing blue jeans?
STUDENT B: Some of us are wearing blue jeans.

1. How many of the people in this room have (short) hair?
2. How many of the students in this class have red grammar books?
3. How many of us are sitting down?
4. How many of your classmates are from (*name of a country*)?
5. How many of the people in this room can speak Chinese?
6. How many of the women in this room are wearing earrings? How many of the men?
7. What are some of your favorite TV programs?
8. How many of the people in this city are friendly?
9. How many of the married women in your country work outside the home?

❑ **Exercise 33. Looking at grammar.** (Charts 14-5 and 14-6)

Choose the correct sentence in each group.

1. a. Some of furniture is old.
   b. Some of the furniture are old.
   c. Some of the furniture is old.

2. a. Some of the coins are valuable.
   b. Some of coins are valuable.
   c. Some of the coin are valuable.

3. a. All of people look happy.
   b. All of the people looks happy.
   c. All of the people look happy.

4. a. Almost all of the students are absent.
   b. Almost all of students are absent.
   c. Almost all of the students is absent.

5. a. Half of homework is due.
   b. Half of the homework is due.
   c. Half of the homework are due.

6. a. Half of the assignments is due.
   b. Half of assignments are due.
   c. Half of the assignments are due.

7. a. Most of the apartments is empty.
   b. Most of the apartments are empty.
   c. Most of apartments are empty.

❑ **Exercise 34. Warm-up.** (Chart 14-7)

Complete the sentences with words that make sense. Are the verbs (in red) singular or plural?

1. After a rain shower, every street is _____.

2. During a snowstorm, everything looks _____.

3. In the summer, everybody likes _____.

14-7 Using *Every, Everyone, Everybody, Everything*

(a) ***Every student** has a book.* (b) ***All of the students** have books.* INCORRECT: *Every of the students has a book.* INCORRECT: *Every students have books.*	Examples (a) and (b) have essentially the same meaning. Note the following pattern: In (a): ***every** + **singular** noun + **singular** verb*
	***Every** is not immediately followed by **of**.* ***Every** is immediately followed by a **singular** noun, as in (a), NOT a plural noun.*
(c) ***Everyone** has a book.* (d) ***Everybody** has a book.*	Examples (c) and (d) have the same meaning. ***Everyone** and **everybody** are followed by a **singular** verb.* Example (c) is more common in writing. Example (d) is more common in speaking.*
(e) *I looked at **everything** in the museum.* (f) ***Everything** is okay.*	In (e): ***everything** = each thing* In (f): ***Everything** is followed by a **singular** verb.*

* In general, indefinite pronouns with *one* are more common in writing. Indefinite pronouns with *body* are more common in speaking.

❏ **Exercise 35. Looking at grammar.** (Chart 14-7)

Choose the correct completion.

1. All of the _____*books*_____ on this desk _____*are*_____ mine.
                         book / books   is / are

2. Every _____ on this desk _____ mine.
                    book / books   is / are

3. All of the _____ _____ here today.
                          student / students   is / are

4. Every _____ _____ here today.
                  student / students   is / are

5. Every _____ at my college _____ tests regularly.
                  teacher / teachers   gives / give

6. All of the _____ at my college _____ a lot of tests.
                       teacher / teachers   gives / give

7. Every _____ in the world _____ bedtime stories.
                    child / children   likes / like

8. All of the _____ in the world _____ that story.
                     child / children   knows / know

9. All of the _____ in this class _____ studying English.
      person / people   is / are

10. Everyone in this class _____ to learn English.
                              wants / want

11. _____ all of the _____ in this class speak English well?
      Does / Do   student / students

12. _____ every _____ in the world like to listen to music?
      Does / Do   person / people

13. _____ all of the _____ in the world like to dance?
      Does / Do   person / people

14. Every _____ in Sweden _____ a good transportation system.
            city / cities   has / have

15. _____ everybody in the world have enough to eat?
      Does / Do

❏ **Exercise 36. Warm-up.** (Chart 14-8)
Read the conversation. Can you figure out the answer to the mystery?

A mystery

   A: Here's a puzzle. See if you can solve it.

   B: Okay.

   A: Victor was standing in his kitchen and looking out the window. It was night. He knew that someone was in the house. He knew that somebody was coming up behind him. How did he know?

   B: Did he hear anyone?

   A: No, he didn't hear anybody.

   B: Did he see someone behind him?

   A: Well, he never turned around.

   B: I know! He smelled someone!

   A: No, sorry.

   B: Did his dog bark?

   A: Victor doesn't have a dog.

   B: I have no idea.

14-8 Indefinite Pronouns: *Something, Someone, Somebody, Anything, Anyone, Anybody*

AFFIRMATIVE STATEMENT	(a) Mari bought *something*. (b) Mari saw *someone*. (c) Mari saw *somebody*.	In affirmative sentences, a form of *some* is used: *something*, *someone*, or *somebody*. *Someone* and *somebody* have the same meaning. *Somebody* is more common in speaking.
NEGATIVE STATEMENT	(d) Joe didn't buy *anything*. (e) Joe didn't see *anyone*. (f) Joe didn't see *anybody*.	In negative sentences, a form of *any* is used: *anything*, *anyone*, or *anybody*. *Anyone* and *anybody* have the same meaning. *Anybody* is more common in speaking.

QUESTION	(g) Did Sam buy *something*?
	(h) Did Sam buy *anything*?
	(i) Did Sam see *someone*?
	(j) Did Sam see *anyone*?
	(k) Did Sam see *somebody*?
	(l) Did Sam see *anybody*?
		In questions, a form of *some* or *any* is used:
		    something/anything,
		    someone/anyone, OR
		    somebody/anybody.

❑ **Exercise 37. Looking at grammar.** (Chart 14-8)
Choose the correct completions. Sometimes both answers are correct.

1. A: Who are you going to work with on the project?
   B: I'm not going to work with ____.
   (a.) anyone   (b.) anybody

2. A: What do you need from the store?
   B: I don't need ____.
   a. someone   b. anything

3. A: Did Thomas talk to ____ at the party?
   B: No, he was really quiet.
   a. somebody   b. someone

4. A: Do you have ____ for me?
   B: Yes, you need to sign these papers.
   a. anything   b. anybody

5. A: You dropped ____.
   B: Oh, my keys. Thanks!
   a. anything   b. something

6. A: ____ called, but I don't remember who or why.
   B: You need to write messages down!
      a. Somebody   b. Anyone

7. A: I have ____ for you: a dozen roses.
   B: For me? Why?
   A: It's our anniversary. Did you forget?
      a. something   b. someone

8. A: Listen! Someone's outside.
   B: I don't see ____.
      a. anyone   b. anybody

❑ **Exercise 38. Looking at grammar.** (Chart 14-8)
Complete the sentences. Use *something*, *someone*, *somebody*, *anything*, or *anyone*, *anybody*.

1. I have _____ *something* _____ in my pocket.

2. Do you have _____ in your pocket?

3. Ryan doesn't have _____ in his pocket.

4. I bought _____ when I went shopping yesterday.

5. Bianca didn't buy _____ when she went shopping.

6. Did you buy _____ when you went shopping?

7. My roommate is talking to _____ on the phone.

8. Kyoko didn't tell _____ her secret.

9. I didn't meet _____ last night.

10. I talked to _____ at the electric company about my bill.

11. Did you talk to _____ about your problem?

12. Carla gave me _____ for my birthday.

13. Frank didn't give me _____ for my birthday.

14. Did Frank give you _____ for your birthday?

15. My brother is sitting at his desk. He's writing an email to _____.

16. The hall is empty. I don't see _____.

17. A: Listen. Do you hear a noise?

   B: No, I don't. I don't hear _____.

18. A: Did you talk to Jim on the phone last night?

   B: No. I didn't talk to _____.

19. A: Where's your bike?

   B: _____ stole it.

20. A: What did you do last weekend?

   B: I didn't do _____. I stayed home.

21. A: Does _____ have some change? I don't have enough for the vending machine. I want to get _____ to eat.

   B: Here.

   A: Thanks. I'll pay you back later.

a vending machine

❑ **Exercise 39. Looking at grammar.** (Chart 14-8)

Your teacher will ask you questions. Answer in complete sentences. Use *anything*, *anyone*, or *anybody*. Close your book for this activity.

1. Close your eyes. Who do you see?

2. Cover your ears. Who do you hear?

3. Close your eyes. What do you see?

4. Cover your ears. What do you hear?

5. You have no money. What are you going to buy at the store?

6. A little boy is holding a candy bar behind his back. His mother asks, "What do you have?" He doesn't want to tell the truth. What does he say?

7. A little girl hits her baby sister, and the baby starts crying. Her mother asks, "What did you do?" She doesn't want to tell the truth. What does she say?

❑ **Exercise 40. Listening.** (Charts 14-5 → 14-8)

Listen to each sentence and choose *yes* or *no*.

Example: You will hear: Someone is wearing sunglasses.
            You will choose: (yes)   no

1. yes   no   3. yes   no   5. yes   no
2. yes   no   4. yes   no   6. yes   no

❑ **Exercise 41. Looking at grammar.** (Chapter 14)

Choose the correct completion.

1. The teacher gave a test paper to every _____ in the class.
   a. student   c. of student
   b. students   d. of students

2. Ariana is a _____ woman.
   a. beautiful Mexican young   c. Mexican beautiful young
   b. beautiful young Mexican   d. young beautiful Mexican

3. _____ the students in our class have dark hair.
   a. All most of   c. Almost
   b. Almost of   d. Almost all of

4. I had some _____ soup for lunch.
   a. vegetable good   c. good vegetable
   b. good vegetables   d. vegetables good

5. The flowers _____.
   a. looked beautiful   c. beautiful look
   b. looked beautifully   d. beautifully look

6. _____ have jobs after school.
   a. A lots of students   c. A lot of students
   b. A lot students   d. A lot student

7. I didn't talk to _____.
   a. something   c. anything
   b. anyone   d. somebody

❑ **Exercise 42. Let's talk.** (Chapter 14)

Work in pairs or small groups. Read the facts about eight friends.

Facts:

- Jack, Jim, Jake, John, Jill, Julie, Joan, and Jan are all friends.
- Two of them are secretly engaged.
- They met five months ago.
- They are going to get married next year.

Who is engaged? Read the clues to find out. (Be careful! Some of the clues are only additional information. They will not help you find the answer.)

Fill in the chart as you work through the clues to solve the puzzle.

Engaged	Jack	Jim	Jake	John	Jill	Julie	Joan	Jan
yes								
no						*X*		

Clues:

1. For Julie's wedding next month, she is going to wear her mother's long white wedding dress. Her mother wore it 30 years ago.

   → *Julie's wedding is next month. The engaged couple is getting married next year, so it's not Julie.*

2. Joan's husband is working in another city right now. They hope to see each other soon.
3. Jill and Jack love each other. They met at Jill's sister's wedding.
4. Jill's sister got married a year ago.
5. Jim is the only computer science student in the group.
6. Joan is a computer science teacher. She began teaching two years ago.
7. Jan's boyfriend is a medical student.
8. All of the friends think Julie is very funny.
9. John loves Jan, but she doesn't love him. He's a friend to her, not a boyfriend.

❑ **Exercise 43. Check your knowledge.** (Chapter 14)

Correct the mistakes.

     wants *happy*
1. Everybody ~~want~~ to be ~~happily~~.

2. I didn't see nobody at the mall.

3. At the library, you need to do your work quiet.

4. I walk in the park every days.

5. Mr. Spencer teaches English very good.

6. The answer looks clearly. Thank you for explaining it.

7. Every grammar test have a lot of difficult questions.

8. I work hard every days.

9. We saw a pretty flowers garden in the park.

10. Galina drives a blue small car.

11. Every of students in the class have a grammar book.

12. The work will take a long time. We can't finish every things today.

13. Everybody in the world want peace.

❏ **Exercise 44. Reading and writing.** (Chapter 14)
Part I. Read the passage.

Ways to Create Happiness

Can money buy happiness? Some psychologists try to answer this question. They do "happiness research." One answer they found is that we can create happiness with memories. We can "buy" memories, and we don't need to spend a lot of money. They believe that simple things in life can create a lot of wonderful memories. Here are some suggestions they give.

- Take someone in your family to a sports event, such as a soccer match or a baseball game.
- Go camping with family or friends.
- Celebrate something important like graduation.
- Have a meal at a restaurant with family and friends.

It's also important to do something to save these special memories. One way is with photos, postcards, or souvenirs. When you see these items later, they will remind you of the fun times you had.

Part II. Write one or more paragraphs about a way you can create special memories with someone. Answer these questions in your paragraph(s). (See the writing sample on the next page.)

1. Who is the person (or people)?
2. What do you like to do together and why?
3. How do you remember your time with this person?

Two Simple Ways I Create Special Memories

     I like to spend time with my parents. They are elderly, and they don't drive anymore. We do a few simple things together.

     I sometimes go with them for walks. They live in the city, and we like to take walks in the park. I tell them about my week and my plans. They like to hear about my life. We walk for about an hour and enjoy the easy exercise.

     I also like to have meals with my parents. Sometimes we go out to a local restaurant. Other times I bring them food from a favorite restaurant or deli.* I buy a nice lunch or dinner, and we eat it at their apartment. Sometimes there is a sports show on TV. We talk about the show while we are eating our meal. We have good memories of our time together.

Part III. Editing check: Work individually or change papers with a partner. Check (✓) for the following:

1. ____ indented paragraph
2. ____ capital letter at the beginning of each sentence
3. ____ period at the end of each sentence
4. ____ use of adjectives and adverbs
5. ____ correct word order for adjectives and adverbs
6. ____ correct spelling (use a dictionary or computer spell-check)

---

deli = delicatessen: a store that sells meats and cheeses, and also makes sandwiches, salads, and soups

Chapter 15
Making Comparisons

❑ **Exercise 1. Warm-up.** (Chart 15-1)
Check (✓) the true sentences.

1. _____ Josh is taller than Lisa.

2. _____ Lisa is taller than Josh.

3. _____ Josh is older than Lisa.

Lisa   Josh

15-1 The Comparative: Using *-er* and *More*

Mary is 25 years old.
John is 20 years old.

(a) Mary is *older than* John.
(b) Health is *more important than* money.

INCORRECT: Mary is more old than John.
INCORRECT: Health is importanter than money.

When we use adjectives (e.g., *old, important*) to compare two people or two things, the adjectives have special forms.

In (a): We add *-er* to an adjective, OR
In (b): We use *more* in front of an adjective.
The use of *-er* or *more* is called the COMPARATIVE FORM.

Notice in the examples: *than* follows the comparative form (*older than*, more important *than*).

	ADJECTIVE	COMPARATIVE	
ADJECTIVES WITH ONE SYLLABLE	**big** **cheap** **old**	**bigger** **cheaper** **older**	Add *-er* to one-syllable adjectives. Spelling note: If an adjective ends in one vowel and one consonant, double the consonant: *big–bigger, fat–fatter, hot–hotter, thin–thinner.*
ADJECTIVES THAT END IN -Y	**funny** **pretty**	**funnier** **prettier**	If an adjective ends in *-y*, change the *-y* to *-i* and add *-er.*
ADJECTIVES WITH TWO OR MORE SYLLABLES	**famous** **important** **interesting**	**more famous** **more important** **more interesting**	Use *more* in front of adjectives that have two or more syllables (except adjectives that end in *-y*).
IRREGULAR COMPARATIVE FORMS	**good** **bad** **far**	**better** **worse** **farther/further**	The comparative forms of *good*, *bad*, and *far* are irregular.

er/more

Vowl
a - e - i - o - u - y → sometime

□ **Exercise 2. Looking at grammar.** (Chart 15-1)
Write the comparative form for these adjectives.

1. old ___older than___

2. small ___smaller___

3. big ___bigger___

4. important ___more important___

5. easy ___more easy___

6. difficult ___more difficult___

7. long ___longer___

8. heavy ___heavier___

9. expensive ___more expensive___

10. sweet ___sweeter___

11. hot ___hotter___

12. good ___better___

13. bad ___worse___

14. far ___farther___

□ **Exercise 3. Looking at grammar.** (Chart 15-1)
Complete the sentences. Use the comparative form of the given words.

1. comfortable   A mattress is ___more comfortable than___ a floor.

2. deep   The Pacific Ocean is ___deeper than___ the Mediterranean Sea.

3. important   Love is ___more important than___ money.

4. lazy   I'm ___lazier than___ my roommate.

5. tall   My brother is ___taller than___ I am.*

6. heavy   Iron is ___heavier than___ wood.

---

*Formal written English: *My brother is taller than I (am).*
Informal spoken English: *My brother is taller than me.*

7. difficult   My physics course is _____more difficult than_____

               my math course.

8. hot   Thailand is a __ˡ hotter__ country __than__ Korea.

9. thin   A giraffe's neck is __thinner than__ an elephant's neck.

10. warm   It's __warmer__ today __than__ yesterday.

11. good   Natasha's English is __better than__ her husband's.

12. long   The Nile River is __longer than__ the Mississippi.

13. intelligent   A dog is __more intelligent than__ a chicken.

14. short   My little finger is __shorter than__ my middle finger.

15. bad   The weather yesterday was __worse than__ it is today.

16. far   Your apartment is __father__ from school

          __than__ mine.

17. strong   A horse is __stronger than__ a person.

18. curly   Jake's hair is __curlier than__ mine.

19. nervous   The groom was __more nervous__ at the wedding

          __than__ the bride.

20. happy   The bride looked __happier than__ the groom.

21. uncomfortable   The groom looked __more uncomfortable__

          the bride.

❑ **Exercise 4. Let's talk: pairwork.** (Chart 15-1)
Work with a partner. Use the adjective in parentheses to compare each pair of items. Use *more* or *-er*.

Example: a mouse, an elephant (small)
→ A mouse is smaller than an elephant.

PARTNER A	PARTNER B
1. a bus, car (big)	1. this book, that one (good)
2. my old shoes, my new shoes (comfortable)	2. my hair, her hair (curly)
3. your hair, my hair (dark)	3. her hair, his hair (straight)
4. my arm, your arm (long)	4. the weather here, the weather in my hometown (bad)
5. biology, chemistry (interesting)	5. this chapter, Chapter 10 (easy)
6. I, my friend (happy)	6. Japanese grammar, English grammar (difficult)

❑ **Exercise 5. Let's talk: class activity.** (Chart 15-1)
Your teacher will put several different books in a central place. Compare one to another using the given adjectives.

Example: big
Response: This book is bigger than that book/that one.

1. large	5. difficult	9. expensive
2. interesting	6. easy	10. cheap
3. small	7. good	11. thick
4. heavy	8. bad	12. important

❑ **Exercise 6. Listening.** (Chart 15-1)
Listen to each sentence. Choose the adjective you hear.

Example: You will hear: Sky Airlines is cheaper than World Airlines.
You will choose: cheap (cheaper)

1. cold	colder	7. safe	safer
2. cold	colder	8. safe	safer
3. cold	colder	9. safe	safer
4. happy	happier	10. fresh	fresher
5. happy	happier	11. funny	funnier
6. happy	happier	12. funny	funnier

❏ **Exercise 7. Looking at grammar.** (Chart 15-1)
Complete the sentences. Use the comparative form of the words from the box or your own words.

big	cold	expensive	hot	large
bright	comfortable	fast	important	sweet
cheap	easy	high	intelligent	warm

1. A bear is ___*bigger than / larger than*___ a mouse.

2. A lemon is sour. An orange is _____ a lemon.

3. The weather today is _____ it was yesterday.

4. When Mrs. Vallero's feet hurt, she wears tennis shoes. Tennis shoes are

   _____ high heels.

a high heel

a tennis shoe

5. I can afford a radio but not a TV. A radio is _____

   _____ a TV.

6. An airplane moves quickly. An airplane is _____ a car.

7. A person can think logically. A person is _____

   an animal.

8. Hills are low. Mountains are _____ hills.

9. The sun gives off a lot of light. The sun is _____ the moon.

10. A motorcycle costs a lot of money. A motorcycle is _____

    _____ a bike.

11. Arithmetic isn't difficult. Arithmetic is _____ algebra.

12. Good health is _____ money.

❑ **Exercise 8. Let's talk.** (Chart 15-1)
Work in pairs, in groups, or as a class. Make comparisons.

Example: feathers to rocks
    → *Feathers are lighter than rocks.* OR
    Rocks are heavier than feathers.

1. an orange to a lemon
2. a lake to an ocean
3. good health to money
4. an airplane to a car
5. a person to an animal
6. the sun to the moon
7. dust to sand
8. arithmetic to algebra
9. bedroom slippers to high heels
10. a giraffe to a person
11. your little finger to your ring finger
12. your ring finger to your thumb
13. love to money
14. a picture from a camera and a picture from a smartphone
15. emailing to texting
16. the weather today to the weather yesterday

❑ **Exercise 9. Let's talk: small groups.** (Chart 15-1)
Work in small groups. Agree or disagree with the statements. Discuss your answers.

In general,

1. women are stronger than men (physically).	yes	no
2. women are stronger than men (emotionally).	yes	no
3. girls are better students than boys.	yes	no
4. strict parents raise better children than lenient* parents.	yes	no
5. relaxed teachers are better than serious teachers.	yes	no
6. cats make better pets than dogs.	yes	no
7. understanding English is harder than speaking it.	yes	no
8. writing English is easier than reading it.	yes	no

*lenient = not strict; not so many rules

❏ **Exercise 10. Let's talk: pairwork.** (Chart 15-1)
Work in pairs. Make comparisons.
   Partner A: Ask your partner a question. Your book is open.
   Partner B: Answer in a complete sentence. Your book is closed.

Example: Name something that is sweeter than an apple.
PARTNER A: What's sweeter than an apple?
PARTNER B: Candy is sweeter than an apple.

1. Name a country that is larger than Mexico.
2. Name a planet that is closer to the sun than the Earth.
3. Name someone who is younger than I am or you are.
4. Name an animal that is more dangerous than a wild dog.
5. Name a bird that is larger than a chicken.
6. Name something that is more expensive than a Mercedes car.
7. Name a sport that is more popular internationally than baseball.
8. Name someone who is more famous than me.

Change roles.
9. Name someone who is taller than you.
10. Name something that is more interesting than basic arithmetic.
11. Name an ocean that is smaller than the Pacific Ocean.
12. Name a place that is farther away from school than your home is.
13. Name an animal that is stronger than a sheep.
14. Name a sport that, in your opinion, is more exciting than golf.
15. Name a place that is colder than this city.
16. Name a place that is more beautiful than this city.

❏ **Exercise 11. Warm-up.** (Chart 15-2)
Which statements do you agree with?

1. Rome is the prettiest city in the world.   yes   no

2. Tokyo is the most expensive city in the world.   yes   no

3. New York is the most exciting city in the world.   yes   no

15-2 The Superlative: Using -est and Most

(a) COMPARATIVE My thumb is **shorter than** my index finger.	The comparative (**-er/more**) compares two things or people.
(b) SUPERLATIVE My hand has five fingers. My thumb is **the shortest** (finger) of all.	The superlative (**-est/most**) compares three or more things or people.

	ADJECTIVE	COMPARATIVE	SUPERLATIVE
ADJECTIVES WITH ONE SYLLABLE	**old** **big***	**older** (than) **bigger** (than)	**the oldest** (of all) **the biggest** (of all)
ADJECTIVES THAT END IN -Y	**pretty** **easy**	**prettier** (than) **easier** (than)	**the prettiest** (of all) **the easiest** (of all)
ADJECTIVES WITH TWO OR MORE SYLLABLES	**expensive** **important**	**more expensive** (than) **more important** (than)	**the most expensive** (of all) **the most important** (of all)
IRREGULAR FORMS	**good** **bad** **far**	**better** (than) **worse** (than) **farther/further** (than)	**the best** (of all) **the worst** (of all) **the farthest/furthest** (of all)

* Spelling note: If an adjective ends in one vowel and one consonant, double the consonant to form the superlative: *big-biggest, fat-fattest, hot-hottest, thin-thinnest.*

❑ **Exercise 12. Looking at grammar.** (Charts 15-1 and 15-2)
Write the comparative and superlative forms of the given adjectives.

		COMPARATIVE	SUPERLATIVE
1.	long	*longer than*	*the longest*
2.	small	Smaller than	the smallest
3.	heavy	heavier than	
4.	comfortable	more comfortable	
5.	hard	harder than	
6.	difficult		
7.	easy		
8.	good		
9.	hot		
10.	cheap		

11. interesting _____ _____

12. pretty _____ _____

13. far _____ _____

14. strong _____ _____

15. bad _____ _____

❑ **Exercise 13. Looking at grammar.** (Charts 15-1 and 15-2)
Complete the sentences. Use the comparative or superlative form of the given adjectives.

1. large <u>   *The largest*   </u> city in Canada is Toronto.

2. long The Nile is _____ river in the world.

3. interesting I'm taking four classes. My history class is _____

_____ of all.

4. high Mt. McKinley in Alaska is _____ mountain in
North America.

5. tall The Sears Tower is _____ building in Chicago.

6. big Lake Superior is _____ lake in North America.

7. short February is _____ month of the year.

8. fast The _____ way to travel is by airplane.

9. far Neptune is _____ planet from the sun.

10. beautiful In my opinion, Montreal and Vancouver are _____

_____ cities in Canada.

11. famous The Gateway Arch is _____
landmark in St. Louis, Missouri.

12. good   In my opinion, Café Fresh has _____ food in
                the city.

13. large   Asia is _____ continent in the world.

14. comfortable Theo is sitting in _____
                chair in the room.

15. good   When you feel sad, laughter is _____ medicine.

16. small   Australia is _____ continent in the world.

17. expensive   Gina ordered _____ food on the menu
                for dinner last night.

18. easy   Taking a taxi is _____ way to get to the airport.

19. important   I think good health is _____
                thing in life.

20. bad   In my opinion, Harry's Steak House is _____
                restaurant in the city.

❏ **Exercise 14. Listening.** (Charts 15-1 and 15-2)

Look at the people in the picture and listen to each sentence. Choose the correct answer.

Example: You will hear: Selena is the youngest.
          You will choose: yes   (no)

Selena   Alberto   Rudy
(18 years old) (60 years old)   (15 years old)

1. yes no	6. yes no
2. yes no	7. yes no
3. yes no	8. yes no
4. yes no	9. yes no
5. yes no	10. yes no

❑ **Exercise 15. Looking at grammar.** (Charts 15-1 and 15-2)

Work in small groups or as a class. Make comparisons about each group of pictures.

A. COMPARE THE SIZES OF THE THREE BALLS.

1. The golf ball is _____*smaller than*_____ the baseball.

2. The soccer ball is _____*larger than*_____ the baseball.

3. The soccer ball is _____*the largest*_____ of all.

B. COMPARE THE AGES OF THE THREE CHILDREN.

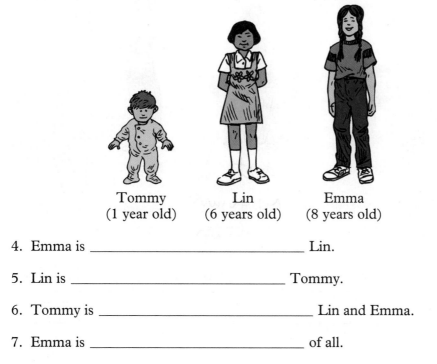

Tommy	Lin	Emma
(1 year old)	(6 years old)	(8 years old)

4. Emma is _____ Lin.

5. Lin is _____ Tommy.

6. Tommy is _____ Lin and Emma.

7. Emma is _____ of all.

C. COMPARE THE HEIGHTS OF THE THREE WOMEN.

Sachi   Karen   Alice

8. _____ is the tallest.

9. _____ is the shortest.

10. _____ is taller than _____ but shorter than

_____.

D. COMPARE THE STRENGTH OF THE THREE MEN.

Brad   Keith   Lars

11. _____

12. _____

13. _____

14. _____

E. COMPARE THE PRICES OF THE THREE VEHICLES.

15. _____

16. _____

17. _____

18. _____

F. COMPARE THE GRADES OF THE THREE TEST PAPERS.

19. _____

20. _____

21. _____

22. _____

G. COMPARE HOW INTERESTING (TO YOU) THE THREE BOOKS LOOK.

23. _____

24. _____

25. _____

26. _____

❑ **Exercise 16. Looking at grammar.** (Charts 15-1 and 15-2)
Complete the sentences. Use the correct form (comparative or superlative) of the given adjectives.

1. long   The Yangtze River is _____longer   than_____ the Mississippi River.

2. long   The Nile is _____the longest_____ river in the world.

3. large   The Caribbean Sea is _____larger   than_____ the Mediterranean Sea.

4. large   The Caribbean Sea is _____the largest_____ sea in the world.

5. high   Mt. Everest is _____the highest_____ mountain in the world.

6. high   Mt. Everest is _____higher   than_____ Mt. McKinley.

7. big   Africa is _____bigger   than_____ North America.

8. small   Europe is _____smaller than_____ South America.

9. large   Asia is _____the largest_____ continent in the world.

10. big   Canada is _____bigger than_____ the United States in area.

11. large   Indonesia is _____larger than_____ Japan in population.

12. good   Fruit is _____better_____ for your health _____than_____ candy.

13. good   The student cafeteria has _____the best_____ roast beef sandwiches in the city.

14. comfortable   I have a pair of boots, a pair of sandals, and a pair of running shoes.

The sandals are ___more comfortable than___

the boots, but the running shoes are ___the most___

___comfortable___ of all.

15. easy   This exercise is ___easier than___ the next one.

16. bad   A: Which is ___worse than___ : a backache or a toothache?

B: I think a toothache is much ___the worst___

a backache.

❑ **Exercise 17. Listening.** (Charts 15-1 and 15-2)
Listen to the sentences about shopping in a clothing store. Write the words you hear.

1. The blue dress ___is more expensive than___ the red one.

2. Well, I think the red one looks _____.

3. Is it too _____, or does it look okay?

4. It's _____ of all the dresses you tried on.

5. I'm not going to buy the brown shoes. They're too _____.

6. This hat is too small. I need a _____ size.

7. Here, this is _____ size they have.

8. I need a belt, but that one is _____ my old one.

9. Is this belt _____ enough?

10. It's perfect. And it's _____ of all of them.

❑ **Exercise 18. Warm-up.** (Chart 15-3)
Complete the sentences with your own words.

1. One of my favorite foods is _____.

2. One of the best movies in theaters right now is _____.

3. One of the hardest classes for me is _____.

4. One of the most interesting cities to visit is _____.

15-3 Using *One Of* + Superlative + Plural Noun

(a) The Amazon is *one of the longest rivers* in the world. INCORRECT: The Amazon is one of the longest river in the world. INCORRECT: The Amazon is one of longest rivers in the world. (b) A Rolls Royce is *one of the most expensive cars* in the world. (c) Alice is *one of the most intelligent people* in our class.	The superlative often follows *one of*. Notice the pattern: **one of** + *superlative* + *plural noun*

❑ **Exercise 19. Looking at grammar.** (Chart 15-3)

Use the given phrases to make sentences. Use *one of* + *superlative* + *plural noun*.

1. a high mountain in the world
   → *Mt. McKinley is one of the highest mountains in the world.*

2. a pretty park in (*the world*)
   → *Monsanto Forest Park in Lisbon is one of the prettiest parks in the world.*

3. a tall person in our class
   → *Talal is one of the tallest people* in our class.*

4. a big city in the world

5. a beautiful place in the world

6. a long river in the world

7. a good restaurant in (*this city*)

8. a famous landmark in the world

9. an important event in the history of the world

❑ **Exercise 20. Let's talk: class interview.** (Chart 15-3)

Walk around the room. Ask and answer questions using *one of* + *superlative* + *plural noun*. Ask two students each question. Write their first names and their answers. Then ask two different students the next question. Share some of their answers with the class.

Example: a big city in Canada
QUESTION: What is one of the biggest cities in Canada?
STUDENT A: Toronto is one of the biggest cities in Canada.
STUDENT B: Vancouver is one of the biggest cities in Canada.

---

* *People* is usually used instead of *persons* in the plural.

	NAME	ANSWER	NAME	ANSWER
1. a big city in Asia				
2. a large state in the United States				
3. a beautiful city in the world				
4. a tall person in our class				
5. a good place to visit in the world				
6. a famous person in the world				
7. an important thing in life				
8. a bad restaurant in (*this city*)				
9. a famous landmark in (*name of a country*)				
10. a tall building in (*name of a city*)				
11. a dangerous sport in the world				
12. a serious problem in the world				

❑ **Exercise 21. Let's talk.** (Charts 15-2 and 15-3)
Work in small groups or as a class. Answer these questions.

1. How many brothers and sisters do you have? Are you the oldest?
2. Who is one of the most famous movie stars in the world?
3. In your opinion, what is the scariest animal in the world?
4. In your opinion, what is one of the most frightening natural events (earthquake, cyclone, volcano, tsunami, etc.)?
5. What is one of the most important inventions in the modern world?
6. What is one of the worst experiences of your life?
7. What are the best things in life?
8. What was the happiest day of your life — or one of the happiest days of your life?
9. Who are the most important people in your life today?

❑ **Exercise 22. Let's talk: small groups.** (Charts 15-1 → 15-3)
First, take the entire quiz by yourself. Circle the letters of the correct answers. If you don't know an answer, guess. Second, form small groups to discuss your answers. You can figure out the correct answers by looking at the *Table of Statistics* on p. 465.

Part I.

1. What is the longest river in the world?
   a. the Yangtze
   b. the Amazon
   c. the Nile
   d. the Mississippi

2. Is the Amazon River longer than the Mississippi River?
   a. yes
   b. no

3. Is the Yangtze River longer than the Mississippi River?
   a. yes
   b. no

4. Which two rivers are almost the same length?
   a. the Nile and the Amazon
   b. the Amazon and the Yangtze
   c. the Nile and the Mississippi
   d. the Mississippi and the Amazon

Part II.

5. What is the largest sea in the world?
   a. the Mediterranean Sea
   b. the South China Sea
   c. the Caribbean Sea

6. Is the South China Sea the smallest of the three seas listed above?
   a. yes
   b. no

Part III.

7. What is the deepest ocean in the world?
   a. the Atlantic Ocean
   b. the Indian Ocean
   c. the Pacific Ocean

8. Is the Indian Ocean larger than the Atlantic Ocean?
   a. yes
   b. no

Part IV.

9. Below is a list of the continents in the world. List them in order according to size, from the largest to the smallest.

Africa   Europe
✓ Antarctica   North America
Asia   South America
Australia

(1) _____ (the largest)

(2) _____

(3) _____

(4) ____Antarctica_____

(5) _____

(6) _____

(7) _____ (the smallest)

Part V

10. Which of the following cities has the largest population in the world?

    a. New York City, U.S.A.   c. Tokyo, Japan

    b. Seoul, South Korea   d. Mexico City, Mexico

11. Is the population of Sao Paulo, Brazil, larger than the population of New York City, U.S.A.?

    a. yes

    b. no

12. Is the population of Sao Paulo, Brazil, larger than the population of Seoul, South Korea?

    a. yes

    b. no

13. What is the largest city in North America?

    a. Mexico City

    b. New York City

Part VI.

14. Which of the following countries has the largest area in the world?

    a. Canada   c. the United States

    b. China   d. Brazil

15. Which of the following two countries is larger in area?

    a. Canada

    b. Brazil

16. Which of the following countries has the largest population in the world?

    a. India   c. the United States

    b. Indonesia   d. China

17. Which of the following two countries has the larger population?

    a. India

    b. Indonesia

18. Which of the following two countries has the larger population?

    a. the United States

    b. Brazil

19. Which of the following two countries has the smaller population?

    a. Egypt

    b. Japan

TABLE OF STATISTICS

PART I.

RIVER	LENGTH
the Amazon River	4,000 miles
the Mississippi River	2,350 miles
the Nile River	4,160 miles
the Yangtze River	3,900 miles

PART II.

SEA	SIZE
the Caribbean Sea	970,000 square miles
the Mediterranean Sea	969,000 square miles
the South China Sea	895,000 square miles

PART III.

OCEAN	SIZE	AVERAGE DEPTH
Atlantic Ocean	31,820,000 square miles	12,100 feet
Indian Ocean	29,000,000 square miles	12,750 feet
Pacific Ocean	64,000,000 square miles	13,000 feet

PART IV.

CONTINENT	SIZE
Africa	12,000,000 square miles
Antarctica	7,000,000 square miles
Asia	17,129,000 square miles
Australia	3,000,000 square miles
Europe	3,837,000 square miles
North America	9,355,000 square miles
South America	6,886,000 square miles

PART V.

CITY	POPULATION*
Mexico City, Mexico	20 million
New York, U.S.A.	21 million
Sao Paulo, Brazil	20 million
Seoul, South Korea	23 million
Tokyo, Japan	37 million

PART VI.

COUNTRY	AREA	POPULATION
Brazil	3,265,059 sq mi	206 million
Canada	3,612,187 sq mi	34 million
China	3,600,927 sq mi	1,343 million*
Egypt	384,000 sq mi	84 million
India	1,147,949 sq mi	1,205 million
Indonesia	767,777 sq mi	248 million
Japan	146,000 sq mi	127 million
the United States	3,539,224 sq mi	314 million

*Approximate population; *1,343 million* is said as "one billion, three hundred forty-three million."

□ **Exercise 23. Reading and grammar.** (Charts 15-1 → 15-3)
Read the story and <u>underline</u> the comparisons. Then answer the question. Give several reasons for your answer. Look at new vocabulary with your teacher first.

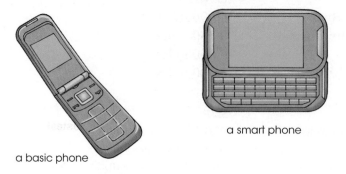

a smart phone

a basic phone

Which Phone?

Jon needs to buy a cell phone. He is trying to decide if he should get a basic phone or a smart phone. His teenage children want him to get a smart phone. They say it is <u>more useful than</u> a basic phone.

> **Do you know these words?**
>
> social media
> Wi-Fi access
> surf the Internet
> eyesight
> QWERTY keyboard
> cool-looking

With a smart phone, Jon can use the Internet to get news and weather, play games, use social media, shop, etc. With a basic phone, Jon can just send voice and text messages and take pictures.

Jon sometimes travels. Right now he uses the Internet on his computer when he has Wi-Fi access. With a smart phone, Jon can always get on the Internet. But he doesn't really like to surf the Internet on a phone screen because his eyesight isn't very good.

John wants to be able to send text messages to his wife and kids. Texting on a smart phone is easier than on a basic phone because a smart phone has a QWERTY keyboard.

Jon doesn't like to spend money. A basic phone is cheaper than a smart phone. Also, the service plan for a basic phone is cheaper.

Jon's kids keep telling him a smart phone is more convenient and modern. They say one of the best things about a smart phone is that it is "cool-looking." Jon doesn't care about that, but in general, he likes to make his children happy.

QUESTION: Which type of phone do you think Jon should buy and why?

□ **Exercise 24. Warm-up.** (Chart 15-4)
Answer the questions.

1. Who speaks English more fluently: you or your teacher?
2. Who speaks your language more slowly: you or someone in your family?
3. Who gets to school earlier: you or a classmate?

15-4 Making Comparisons with Adverbs

	COMPARATIVE	SUPERLATIVE	
(a) Kim speaks *more fluently than* Ali (does). (b) Anna speaks *the most fluently of all*.	more fluently more slowly more quickly	the most fluently the most slowly the most quickly	Use *more* and *most* with adverbs that end in *-ly*.*
(c) Mike worked *harder than* Sam (did). (d) Sue worked *the hardest of all*.	harder faster earlier later	the hardest the fastest the earliest the latest	Use *-er* and *-est* with irregular adverbs: *hard, fast, early, late.*
(e) Rosa writes *better than* I do. (f) Kim writes *the best of all*.	better	the best	*Better* and *best* are forms of the adverb *well.*

*Exception: *early–earlier–the earliest*

❏ **Exercise 25. Looking at grammar.** (Chart 15-4)
Complete the sentences with the correct form (comparative or superlative) of the given adverbs.

1. late   Diana got home ___*later than*___ Claire (did).

2. quickly   I finished my work _____ Jamal (did).

3. beautifully   Zara sings _____ Lila (does).

4. beautifully   Arianna sings _____ of all.

5. hard   My sister works _____ I (do).

6. hard   My brother works _____ of all.

7. carefully   My husband drives _____ I (do).

8. early   We arrived at the party _____ the Smiths (did).

9. early   The Wilsons arrived at the party _____ of all.

10. well   You can write _____ I (can).

11. well   Pavel can write _____ of all.

12. clearly   Larisa pronounces her words _____

     Katerina (does).

13. fluently   Ava speaks Spanish _____ I (do).

14. fluently   Ian speaks Spanish _____ of all.

□ **Exercise 26. Looking at grammar.** (Chart 15-1 → 15-4)
Use the correct form (adjective or adverb, comparative or superlative) of the given words.

1. careful   Molly drives _____*more carefully than her*_____ brother does.

2. beautiful   A tiger is _____ a goat.

3. neat   Yukio's apartment is _____ mine.

4. neat   Henry's apartment is _____ of all.

5. neat   You write _____ I do.

6. neat   Lauren writes _____ of all.

7. clear   This author explains her ideas _____ that author.

8. good   I like rock music _____ classical music.

9. good   My husband can sing _____ I can.

10. good   My daughter can sing _____ of all.

11. late   David usually goes to bed _____ his roommate.

12. clear   Helen pronounces her words _____

of all the students in the class.

13. sharp   A razor is usually _____ a kitchen knife.

14. artistic   My son is _____ my daughter.

15. slow   I eat _____ my husband does.

16. long   Serena has the _____ hair of all the kids in her class.

□ **Exercise 27. Listening.** (Charts 15-1 → 15-4)
Listen to each sentence. Write the words you hear.

1. I work _____*faster than*_____ Alec does.

2. Toshi finished his work _____ of all.

3. Mimi studies _____ Fred.

4. Jean studies _____ of all.

5. Is a motorcycle _____ a bike?

6. Kalil speaks _____ Haruko does.

7. A turtle moves _____ a cat does.

8. This suitcase is _____ that one.

9. My glasses are _____ my contact lenses.

10. I can see _____ with my glasses.

❏ **Exercise 28. Warm-up.** (Chart 15-5)
Agree or disagree with these statements about sports.

a golf club   a baseball bat   a badminton racket

a tennis ball

a tennis racket

a skydiver

a diver

1. Golf is similar to baseball.	yes	no
2. Badminton and tennis are the same.	yes	no
3. Diving is very different from skydiving.	yes	no

15-5 Comparisons: Using *The Same (As)*, *Similar (To)*, and *Different (From)*

THE SAME (AS)	SIMILAR (TO)	DIFFERENT (FROM)
A and B are *the same*. A is *the same as* B.	C and D are *similar*. C is *similar to* D.	E and F are *different*. E is *different from* F.

❏ **Exercise 29. Let's talk: class activity.** (Chart 15-5)
Answer the questions.

1. Are Pictures A and B the same?
2. Are Pictures A and C the same?
3. Are Pictures A and C similar?

4. Are Pictures A and C different?
5. Are Pictures C and D similar?
6. Are Pictures C and D different?

❏ **Exercise 30. Looking at grammar.** (Chart 15-5)
Complete the sentences. Use *the same* (*as*), *similar* (*to*), and *different* (*from*) in your completions.

1. A ___*is the same as*___ F.

2. D and E ___*are similar** OR *are different*___.

3. C _____ D.

---

*Similar gives the idea that two things are the same in some ways (e.g., both D and E have four edges) but different in other ways (e.g., D is a rectangle, and E is a square).

4. B _____ D.

5. B and D _____.

6. C and D _____.

7. A and F _____.

8. F and G _____.

9. F _____ G.

10. G _____ A and F but _____ C.

❏ **Exercise 31. Listening.** (Chart 15-5)

Listen to the comparisons of Pictures A through G in Exercise 30. Are these comparisons correct?

Example: You will hear: A and F are the same.
You will choose: (yes) no

1. yes	no	4. yes	no	6. yes	no
2. yes	no	5. yes	no	7. yes	no
3. yes	no				

❏ **Exercise 32. Let's talk: class activity.** (Chart 15-5)
Answer the questions.

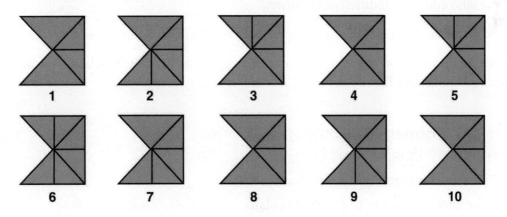

1. Which figures have the same design?
2. Is there at least one figure that is different from all the rest?

Just for fun:

3. How many triangles are there in figure 1? (*Answer: Seven.*)
4. How many triangles are there in figure 2?
5. How many triangles are there in figure 6?

❏ **Exercise 33. Let's talk: class activity.** (Chart 15-5)
Your teacher will ask you questions. Practice using *the same* (*as*), *similar* (*to*), and *different* (*from*). Close your book for this activity.

Example: Look at (. . .)'s clothes and (. . .)'s clothes. What is different about them?
Response: Their shoes are different. (. . .) is wearing running shoes, and (. . .) is wearing sandals.

1. Look around the room. Name things that are the same.

2. Look around the room. Name things that are similar but not the same.

3. Find two pens that are the same length. Find two pieces of paper that are the same size. Find two notebooks that are different sizes.

4. Find two people in the class who are wearing (earrings). Are their (earrings) the same, similar, or different?

5. Who in the class has a (notebook, briefcase, backpack) that is similar to yours? Does anyone have a (notebook, briefcase, backpack) that is the same as yours?

6. Do any of the people in this room have the same hairstyle? Name two people who have similar hairstyles.

7. Whose shirt is the same color as yours today? Name some things in this room that are the same color. Name things that are similar colors.

8. Do any of the people in this room come from the same country? Who? Name two people who come from different countries.

9. Name an animal that is similar to a tiger. Name a bird that is similar to a duck.

10. Are Egypt and Italy on the same continent? Egypt and Algeria? Thailand and South Korea? Mexico and Brazil?

❏ **Exercise 34. Warm-up.** (Chart 15-6)
Which statements do you agree with?

1. a. White chocolate and dark chocolate are alike.

   b. White chocolate is not like dark chocolate.

2. a. Broccoli and cauliflower are alike.

   b. Broccoli is not like cauliflower.

3. a. Towels are like sheets.

   b. Towels and sheets aren't alike.

15-6 Comparisons: Using *Like* and *Alike*

You have a pen with blue ink.
I have a pen with blue ink.
 	
(a) Your pen *is like* my pen.
(b) Your pen and my pen *are alike*.
(c) Our pens *are alike*.
	like = *similar to*
	alike = *similar*
	
	Like and *alike* have the same meaning, but the sentence patterns are different.
	    this + *be* + *like* + *that*
	    this and that + *be* + *alike*

❏ **Exercise 35. Let's talk: pairwork.** (Chart 15-6)

Work with a partner. Take turns making sentences with ***like.*** Check (✓) the things in Column B that compare with the items in Column A. Discuss the ways in which the two things you are comparing are similar.

Example: a pencil, a bus

Column A	Column B
1. a pencil 2. a bus	a glass a human hand ✓ a pen a lemon ✓ a taxi

PARTNER A: A pencil is like a pen in some ways. You can write with both of them. Your turn now.

PARTNER B: A bus is like a taxi. You can ride in both of them. Your turn now.
                Etc.

Column A	Column B
1. a bush 2. a cup 3. a hill 4. honey 5. a monkey's hand 6. an orange 7. an alley 8. a sea 9. a couch 10. a jacket 11. a butterfly	a glass a human hand a lemon a chair a mountain an ocean a street sugar a bird a suit coat a tree

❏ **Exercise 36. Looking at grammar.** (Chart 15-6)
Complete the sentences with *like* and *alike*.

1. You and I have similar books. In other words, your book is _____*like*_____ mine.

   Our books are _____*alike*_____.

2. Mr. Wong and I have similar coats. In other words, Mr. Wong's coat is

   _____ mine. Our coats are _____.

3. Tess and Matt have similar cars. In other words, their cars are _____.

4. You and I have similar hats. In other words, your hat is _____ mine.

5. A town is _____ a city in some ways.

6. A foot and a hand are _____ in some ways but different in other ways.

7. A dormitory and an apartment building are _____ in many ways.

8. A motorcycle is _____ a bike in some ways.

❏ **Exercise 37. Looking at grammar.** (Charts 15-5 and 15-6)
Choose <u>all</u> the completions that are grammatically correct and make sense.

1. French and Spanish are _____.
   a. different from
   b. like
   c. alike
   d. the same
   e. similar

2. French is _____ Spanish.
   a. different from
   b. similar
   c. alike
   d. the same as
   e. similar to

3. Coffee tastes _____ lemonade.
   a. different
   b. similar to
   c. the same as
   d. different from
   e. like

4. Fog and smog sometimes look _____.
   a. similar to
   b. similar
   c. like
   d. different from
   e. alike

❏ **Exercise 38. Warm-up.** (Chart 15-7)
Complete the sentences. Give your opinion.

1. The weather in _____ is often cold and wet, but the weather in
                    (*name of a country*)

   _____ is often warm and clear.
        (*name of a country*)

2. _____ is a great place for a vacation, but _____ is
   (*name of a city*)   (*name of a city*)

   a boring place to visit.

15-7 Using *But*

(a) John is rich, ***but*** Mary is poor.	***But*** gives the idea that "This is the opposite of that."
(b) The weather was cold, ***but*** we were warm inside our house.	A comma comes before ***but*** as in (b), when it introduces a main clause.

❏ **Exercise 39. Looking at grammar.** (Chart 15-7)
Complete the sentences with adjectives.

1. An orange is sweet, but a lemon is _____*sour*_____.

2. The coffee in this cup is hot, but the coffee in that cup is _____.

3. These dishes are clean, but those dishes are _____.

4. This suitcase is heavy, but that suitcase is _____.

5. My hair is light, but my brother's hair is _____.

6. These shoes are uncomfortable, but those shoes are _____.

7. This street is narrow, but that street is _____.

8. This exercise is easy, but that exercise is _____.

9. A chicken is stupid, but a human being is _____.

10. This answer is right, but that answer is _____.

11. This towel is dry, but that towel is _____.

12. This cup is full, but that cup is _____.

13. Those dishcloths are dirty, but these dishcloths are _____.

14. A pillow is soft, but a rock is _____.

❏ **Exercise 40. Listening.** (Chart 15-7)

Listen to each sentence and write an adjective with the opposite meaning.

Example: You will hear: This exercise is easy, but that exercise is . . .

You will write: _____hard_____.

1. _____.

2. _____.

3. _____.

4. _____.

5. _____.

6. _____.

7. _____.

8. _____.

❏ **Exercise 41. Warm-up.** (Chart 15-8)

Are any of these sentences true for you? What do you notice about the verbs in red?

1. I don't study a lot, but my friends do.   T   F

2. I can't fly an airplane, but someone in my family can.   T   F

3. I like rock music, but some of my friends don't.   T   F

4. I will be here next year, but some of my friends won't.   T   F

5. I didn't drive to school today, but my teacher did.   T   F

6. I grew up with a pet, but my parents didn't.   T   F

15-8 Using Verbs after *But*

AFFIRMATIVE VERB + *BUT* + NEGATIVE VERB		Often the verb phrase following *but* is shortened, as in the examples.
(a) John *is* rich,	*but*	Mary *isn't*.
(b) Balls *are* round,	*but*	boxes *aren't*.
(c) I *was* in class,	*but*	Po *wasn't*.
(d) Sue *studies* hard,	*but*	Sam *doesn't*.
(e) We *like* movies,	*but*	they *don't*.
(f) Alex *came,*	*but*	Maria *didn't*.
(g) People *can* talk,	*but*	animals *can't*.
(h) Olga *will* be there,	*but*	Ivan *won't*.
NEGATIVE VERB + *BUT* + AFFIRMATIVE VERB		
(i) Mary *isn't* rich,	*but*	John *is*.
(j) Boxes *aren't* round,	*but*	balls *are*.
(k) Po *wasn't* in class,	*but*	I *was*.
(l) Sam *doesn't* study,	*but*	Sue *does*.
(m) They *don't* like cats,	*but*	we *do*.
(n) Maria *didn't* come,	*but*	Alex *did*.
(o) Animals *can't* talk,	*but*	people *can*.
(p) Ivan *won't* be there,	*but*	Olga *will*.

❏ **Exercise 42. Looking at grammar.** (Chart 15-8)
Complete each sentence with an appropriate verb, affirmative or negative.

1. Lana is at home, but her husband _____*isn't*_____ .

2. Hiroki isn't at home, but his wife _____ .

3. Beds are comfortable, but park benches _____ .

4. I wasn't at home last night, but my roommate _____ .

5. Fran was in class yesterday, but Irena and Maggie _____ .

6. I don't want to go to the movie, but my friends _____ .

7. Tariq can speak French, but I _____ .

8. Leah will be at the meeting, but Evelyn _____ .

9. This shirt is clean, but that one _____ .

10. These shoes aren't comfortable, but those shoes _____ .

11. Ethan doesn't write clearly, but Andrew _____ .

12. I ate breakfast this morning, but my roommate _____ .

13. Carol has a car, but Jerry _____ .

14. Jerry doesn't have a car, but Carol _____ .

15. Ron was at the party, but his wife _____ .

16. Ron went to the party, but his wife _____ .

17. Boris can't speak Spanish, but his wife _____ .

18. I won't be at home tonight, but Mia _____ .

19. Liam will be in class tomorrow, but Tyler _____ .

20. Olivia won't be here tomorrow, but Renata _____ .

21. The hotel wasn't expensive, but the plane tickets _____ .

22. Evan is going to graduate on time, but his twin bother _____ .

23. Gabrielle doesn't know how to drive yet, but her friends _____ .

24. I have to work late tonight, but my co-workers _____ .

❏ **Exercise 43. Listening.** (Chart 15-8)

Listen to the sentences. Complete each sentence with an appropriate verb, affirmative or negative.

Example: You will hear: The students wanted to play a vocabulary game, but their teacher . . .

You will write: _____*didn't*_____ .

1. _____ .

2. _____ .

3. _____ .

4. _____ .

5. _____ .

6. _____ .

7. _____ .

8. _____ .

9. _____ .

10. _____ .

❏ **Exercise 44. Let's talk: class activity.** (Chart 15-8)

Your teacher will ask you questions. Answer them using **but**. Close your book for this activity.

Example: Who in the class was at home last night? Who wasn't at home last night?
TEACHER: Who was at home last night?
STUDENT A: I was.
TEACHER: Who wasn't at home last night?
STUDENT B: I wasn't at home last night.
TEACHER: (*to Student C*) Summarize, using *but*.
STUDENT C: (*Student A*) was at home last night, but (*Student B*) wasn't.

1. Who wears glasses? Who doesn't wear glasses?

2. Who is married? Who isn't married?

3. Who didn't watch TV last night? Who watched TV last night?

4. Who will be in class tomorrow? Who won't be in class tomorrow?

5. Who has a pet? Who doesn't have a pet?

6. Who studied last night? Who didn't study last night?

7. Who can play (*a musical instrument*)? Who can't play (*that musical instrument*)?

8. Who is hungry right now? Who isn't hungry right now?

9. Who lives in an apartment? Who doesn't live in an apartment?

10. Who doesn't drink coffee? Who drinks coffee?

11. Who won't be at home tonight? Who will be at home tonight?

12. Who was in class yesterday? Who wasn't in class yesterday?

13. Who can't speak (*a language*)? Who can speak (*a language*)?

14. Who didn't stay home last night? Who stayed home last night?

15. Who has _____? Who doesn't have _____?

❏ **Exercise 45. Let's talk: pairwork.** (Chart 15-8)
Work with a partner. Picture A and Picture B are not the same. There are many
differences between them. Can you find all of the differences? Take turns pointing out the
differences.

Example:
PARTNER A: The woman is sitting in Picture A, but she's lying down in Picture B.
Your turn now.
PARTNER B: There's a small fish in Picture A but a large fish in Picture B.
Your turn now.
Etc.

Picture A

Picture B

❏ **Exercise 46. Let's talk: pairwork.** (Chapter 15)

Work with a partner.

    Partner A: Ask Partner B questions. Your book is open.
    Partner B: Answer in complete sentences. Your book is closed.

1. What's the longest river in the world?*
2. What's the biggest continent? What's the second biggest continent?
3. What country has the largest population?
4. Is a square the same as a rectangle?
5. Name a country that is farther south than Mexico.
6. Name an animal that is similar to a horse.
7. Name a place that is noisier than a library.
8. Is a dormitory like an apartment building? How are they different/similar?
9. Is (. . .)'s grammar book different from yours?
10. What is one of the most famous landmarks in the world?

Change roles.

11. Is the population of Seoul, South Korea, larger or smaller than the population of São Paulo, Brazil?
12. Is the Atlantic Ocean deeper than the Indian Ocean?
13. What's the smallest continent in the world?
14. Name two students in this class who speak the same native language. Do they come from the same country?
15. Look at all the desks in the classroom. Are they different? How?
16. Is a lake like a river? How are they different? How are they similar?
17. Name an insect that is smaller than a bee.
18. Name a city that is farther north than Rome, Italy.
19. What is the most popular sport in your country?
20. What is one of the most important inventions in the modern world? Why is it more important than (*name of another invention*)?

❏ **Exercise 47. Looking at grammar.** (Chapter 15)

Choose the correct completion.

1. A lion is _____ a tiger.
    a. similar   b. similar with   c. similar from   d. similar to

2. Lions and tigers are _____.
    a. the same   b. similar   c. similar to   d. the same as

3. Good health is one of _____ in a person's life.
    a. best thing   c. the best things
    b. the best thing   d. best things

---

*If you need to, look at the *Table of Statistics* on p. 465.

4. There were many chairs in the room. I sat in _____ chair.
   a. the comfortablest   c. most comfortable
   b. the most comfortable   d. more comfortable

5. Jane's story was _____ Jack's story.
   a. funnier than   c. more funnier than
   b. funny than   d. more funny

6. My last name is _____ my cousin's.
   a. same   c. same as
   b. same as   d. the same as

7. I live _____ away from school than you do.
   a. far   b. farther   c. more far   d. farthest

8. Emir speaks _____ than Hamid.
   a. more clearly   c. more clear
   b. clearlier   d. more clearer

9. Roger works hard every day, but his brother _____.
   a. is   b. isn't   c. does   d. doesn't

❏ **Exercise 48. Check your knowledge.** (Chapter 15)
Correct the mistakes.

            harder
1. English is ~~hard, more~~ than my language.

2. A monkey is intelligenter than a cow.

3. My grade on the test was worst from yours. You got a more better grade.

4. Soccer is one of most popular sport in the world.

5. Felix speaks English more fluent than Ernesto.

6. Girls and boys are differents. Girls are different to boys.

7. A rectangle and a square similar.

8. Nola's coat is similar with mine.

9. Victor's coat is same mine.

10. Nicolas and Malena aren't a same height. Nicolas is more tall than Malena.

11. Professor Wilson teaches full-time, but her husband isn't.

12. Your pen, my pen they alike.

13. My cousin is the same age with my brother.

14. What is most pretty place in the world?

15. For me, chemistry most difficult than biology.

❏ **Exercise 49. Reading and writing.** (Chapter 15)

Part I. Read the story.

My Best Friend

My best friend is Jacob. We have an interesting friendship because we are similar and different in several ways.

We like to study, and we are both smart but in different subjects. His math scores are higher than mine, but my language and history grades are better than his.

Physically we are not alike. Jacob is medium height and very athletic. He is stronger than me, and he can run faster than me. I am tall, and I can't lift heavy weights because it hurts my back. I'm also a slower runner than Jacob.

We like to go to sports events together. One of our favorite sports is baseball. We can talk about baseball for hours.

Jacob is quiet, and I am more talkative. Sometimes Jacob says I talk too much, but he laughs when he says it. He is a better listener than me, so people say we make a good pair.

We enjoy our time together. We think this is because we're not the same and we're not really different.

Part II. Write one or more paragraph(s) about you and a friend. Write about your similarities and differences. The box contains comparison words you may want to use in your paragraph.

WORDS USED IN COMPARISONS		
alike	-er/more	similar (to)
but	-est/most	the same (as)
different (from)	like	

Part III. Editing check: Work individually or change papers with a partner. Check (✓) for the following:

1. _____ indented paragraph

2. _____ capital letter at the beginning of each sentence

3. _____ period at the end of each sentence

4. _____ use of **-er/more** for comparing two things

5. _____ use of **the -est/most** for comparing three or more things

6. _____ correct use of **like/alike, similar (to), the same (as), different (from)**

7. _____ correct spelling (use a dictionary or computer spell-check)

Appendix 1
English Handwriting

English Handwriting	
PRINTING	CURSIVE

PRINTING

Aa	Jj	Ss
Bb	Kk	Tt
Cc	Ll	Uu
Dd	Mm	Vv
Ee	Nn	Ww
Ff	Oo	Xx
Gg	Pp	Yy
Hh	Qq	Zz
Ii	Rr	

CURSIVE

Aa	Jj	Ss
Bb	Kk	Tt
Cc	Ll	Uu
Dd	Mm	Vv
Ee	Nn	Ww
Ff	Oo	Xx
Gg	Pp	Yy
Hh	Qq	Zz
Ii	Rr	

Vowels = *a, e, i, o, u*

Consonants = *b, c, d, f, g, h, j, k, l, m, n, p, q, r, s, t, v, w, x, y, z**

*The letter *z* is pronounced "zee" in American English and "zed" in British English.

Appendix 2
Numbers

CARDINAL NUMBERS		ORDINAL NUMBERS	
1	one	1st	first
2	two	2nd	second
3	three	3rd	third
4	four	4th	fourth
5	five	5th	fifth
6	six	6th	sixth
7	seven	7th	seventh
8	eight	8th	eighth
9	nine	9th	ninth
10	ten	10th	tenth
11	eleven	11th	eleventh
12	twelve	12th	twelfth
13	thirteen	13th	thirteenth
14	fourteen	14th	fourteenth
15	fifteen	15th	fifteenth
16	sixteen	16th	sixteenth
17	seventeen	17th	seventeenth
18	eighteen	18th	eighteenth
19	nineteen	19th	nineteenth
20	twenty	20th	twentieth
21	twenty-one	21st	twenty-first
22	twenty-two	22nd	twenty-second
23	twenty-three	23rd	twenty-third
24	twenty-four	24th	twenty-fourth
25	twenty-five	25th	twenty-fifth
26	twenty-six	26th	twenty-sixth
27	twenty-seven	27th	twenty-seventh
28	twenty-eight	28th	twenty-eighth
29	twenty-nine	29th	twenty-ninth
30	thirty	30th	thirtieth
40	forty	40th	fortieth
50	fifty	50th	fiftieth
60	sixty	60th	sixtieth
70	seventy	70th	seventieth
80	eighty	80th	eightieth
90	ninety	90th	ninetieth
100	one hundred	100th	one hundredth
200	two hundred	200th	two hundredth
1,000	one thousand	1,000th	one thousandth
10,000	ten thousand	10,000th	ten thousandth
100,000	one hundred thousand	100,000th	one hundred thousandth
1,000,000	one million	1,000,000th	one millionth

Appendix 3
Ways of Saying Time

9:00   It's nine o'clock.
       It's nine.

9:05   It's nine-oh-five.
       It's five (minutes) after nine.
       It's five (minutes) past nine.

9:10   It's nine-ten.
       It's ten (minutes) after nine.
       It's ten (minutes) past nine.

9:15   It's nine-fifteen.
       It's a quarter after nine.
       It's a quarter past nine.

9:30   It's nine-thirty.
       It's half past nine.

9:45   It's nine-forty-five.
       It's a quarter to ten.
       It's a quarter of ten.

9:50   It's nine-fifty.
       It's ten (minutes) to ten.
       It's ten (minutes) of ten.

12:00 It's noon.
       It's midnight.

A.M. = morning: It's nine A.M.
P.M. = afternoon/evening/night: It's nine P.M.

Appendix 4
Days/Months/Seasons

DAYS	ABBREVIATION	MONTHS	ABBREVIATION	SEASONS*
Monday	Mon.	January	Jan.	winter
Tuesday	Tues.	February	Feb.	spring
Wednesday	Wed.	March	Mar.	summer
Thursday	Thurs.	April	Apr.	fall or autumn
Friday	Fri.	May	May	
Saturday	Sat.	June	Jun.	
Sunday	Sun.	July	Jul.	
		August	Aug.	
		September	Sept.	
		October	Oct.	
		November	Nov.	
		December	Dec.	

*Seasons of the year are only capitalized when they begin a sentence.

WRITING DATES:

Month/Day/Year

10/31/41	= October 31, 1941
4/15/98	= April 15, 1998
7/4/1906	= July 4, 1906
7/4/07	= July 4, 2007

SAYING DATES:

Usual Written Form	Usual Spoken Form
January 1	January first / the first of January
March 2	March second / the second of March
May 3	May third / the third of May
June 4	June fourth / the fourth of June
August 5	August fifth / the fifth of August
October 10	October tenth / the tenth of October
November 27	November twenty-seventh / the twenty-seventh of November

Appendix 5
Supplementary Charts

A5-1 Basic Capitalization Rules

	Use a capital letter for:
(a) Joan and I are friends.	the pronoun "I"
(b) They are late.	the first word of a sentence
(c) Sam Bond and Tom Adams are here.	names of people
(d) Mrs. Peterson Professor Jones Dr. Costa	titles of people*
(e) Monday, Tuesday, Wednesday	the days of the week
(f) April, May, June	the months of the year
(g) New Year's Day	holidays
(h) Los Angeles Florida, Ontario Germany Lake Baikal Amazon River Pacific Ocean Mount Everest Broadway, Fifth Avenue	names of places: cities, states and provinces, countries, lakes, rivers, oceans, mountains, streets
(i) German, Chinese, Swedish	languages and nationalities
(j) Pirates of the Caribbean Romeo and Juliet	the first word of a title, for example, in a book or movie. Capitalize the other words, but not: articles (**the, a, an**), short prepositions (**with, in, at,** etc.), and these words: **and, but, or.**
(k) Buddhism, Christianity, Hinduism, Islam, Judaism	religions

* *Mrs.* = woman: married   *Miss* = woman: unmarried
  Ms. = woman: married or unmarried   *Mr.* = man: married or unmarried

A5-2 Voiceless and Voiced Sounds for *-s* Endings on Verbs

Voiceless	Voiced	
(a) /p/ sleep /t/ write /f/ laugh	(b) /b/ rub /d/ ride /v/ drive	Some sounds are "voiceless." You don't use your voice box. You push air through your teeth and lips. For example, the sound /p/ comes from air through your lips. The final sounds in (a) are voiceless. Common voiceless sounds are *f, k, p, t, sh, ch,* and voiceless *th*.
		Some sounds are "voiced." You use your voice box to make voiced sounds. For example, the sound /b/ comes from your voice box. The final sounds in (b) are voiced. Common voiced sounds are *b, d, g, j, l, m, n, r, v,* and voiced *th*.
(c) sleeps = *sleep*/s/ writes = *write*/s/ laughs = *laugh*/s/	(d) rubs = *rub*/z/ rides = *ride*/z/ drives = *drive*/z/	Final *-s* is pronounced /s/ after voiceless sounds, as in (c). Final *-s* is pronounced /z/ after voiced sounds, as in (d).

I can feel my voice box. It vibrates.

A5-3 Final *-ed* Pronunciation for Simple Past Verbs

Final *-ed* has three pronunciations: /t/, /d/, and /əd/.

End of Verb	Base Form	Simple Past	Pronunciation	
VOICELESS	(a) help laugh wash	helped laughed washed	*help*/t/ *laugh*/t/ *wash*/t/	Final *-ed* is pronounced /t/ if a verb ends in a voiceless sound, as in (a).
VOICED	(b) rub live smile	rubbed lived smiled	*rub*/d/ *live*/d/ *smile*/d/	Final *-ed* is pronounced /d/ if a verb ends in a voiced sound, as in (b).
-d OR *-t*	(c) need want	needed wanted	*need*/əd/ *want*/əd/	Final *-ed* is pronounced /əd/ if a verb ends in the letters *d* or *t*, as in (c).

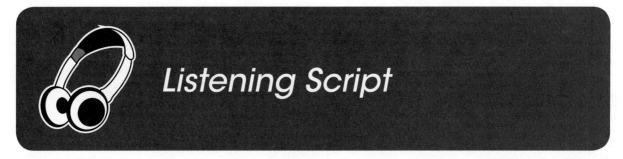

Listening Script

NOTE: You may want to pause the audio after each item or in longer passages so that there is enough time to complete each task.

Exercise 5, p. 267.
1. Where did Sabrina go?
2. Why did Sabrina go there?
3. Where did Isabel go?
4. When did Isabel get there?
5. Why did Isabel go there?
6. Where did Marco go?
7. When did Marco get there?
8. Where did Bill go?
9. What time did Bill get there?

Exercise 7, p. 268.
1. Why did you leave early?
2. Why didn't she help us?
3. Why didn't they believe him?
4. Why did he do that?
5. Why didn't we know about the problem?
6. Why did we come here?
7. Why did I say that?
8. Why didn't I say that?

Exercise 13, p. 271.
1. When did he arrive?
2. Why did you leave?
3. What did she want?
4. Where did you study?
5. What did he say?
6. When did they move?
7. Where did they move to?

Exercise 19, p. 276.
1. When did you leave?
2. Where did Sally meet her husband?
3. What did you need?
4. Where was the party?
5. Why did you move here?

6. Who came late?
7. Why didn't you help?

Exercise 24, p. 279.
1. The student didn't understand . . .
2. The woman spent . . .
3. Did you cut . . .
4. The car hit . . .
5. The man forgot . . .

Exercise 28, p. 281.
1. A tree fell . . .
2. The girls won . . .
3. The teacher drew . . .
4. I felt . . .
5. My brother threw . . .

Exercise 32, p. 283.
1. Mrs. Brown fed . . .
2. Mr. and Mrs. James built . . .
3. The dog bit . . .
4. The children hid . . .
5. The teacher held . . .

Exercise 51, p. 296.
Part III.
1. Steve Jobs was born in 1955.
2. While he was growing up in Palo Alto, California, he became interested in computers.
3. Jobs and Wozniak built their first computer together.
4. After Jobs graduated from high school, he went to Reed College.
5. He wasn't there very long, but he stayed in the area.
6. He learned a lot about calligraphy, and it helped him with the design of his products.
7. In 1985, Apple fired him, so he started NeXT Computer, Incorporated.
8. While he was working at NeXT, he met Laurene Powell, and they got married.
9. Under Jobs, Apple became very successful.

10. Unfortunately, while Jobs was working at Apple, he got cancer.
11. Medical treatments didn't cure him, and Jobs died in 2011.

Chapter 10: Expressing Future Time, Part 1

Exercise 9, p. 308.
1. Look. The doctor is coming.
2. The doctor is coming soon.
3. Oh, no. It's raining.
4. We are leaving early in the morning.
5. Run! The bus is coming.
6. Shh. Class is beginning.
7. We're going to a movie this afternoon.
8. My parents are coming over tonight.

Exercise 11, p. 308.
1. I am leaving soon.
2. Our class starts at nine.
3. Silvia is coming to the meeting tomorrow.
4. The doctor is going to call you.
5. Are you going to study tonight?
6. We are having dinner at a restaurant tomorrow.
7. We aren't going to the concert tonight.
8. Evan always eats a snack at midnight.
9. Who is going to help me?

Exercise 18, p. 312.
1. Maggie is going to the office . . .
2. My boss left . . .
3. The Carlsons got married . . .
4. The store is going to open . . .
5. The movie started . . .
6. We took a vacation . . .
7. Janet is going to graduate . . .
8. I'm going to buy a car . . .
9. There was a meeting at school . . .

Exercise 25, p. 316.
1. Jean is going to leave in a couple of days.
2. Lena is going to leave in a few weeks.
3. We sold our house a couple of years ago.
4. The phone rang a few minutes ago.
5. Marc is going to be here in a few minutes.

Exercise 31, p. 319.
1. They are going to finish this Thursday.
2. They talked about the project this morning.
3. It is going to rain this week.

4. It rained a lot this month.
5. It's raining really hard this week.
6. I am going to graduate from college this year.
7. Suzanne is doing her homework in the library.
8. The professor spoke for two hours this morning.
9. She's going to give us a test this week.
10. We had a lot of homework today.

Exercise 35, p. 320.
Part I.
1. a. The doctor will see you in a few minutes. OR
   b. The doctor'll see you in a few minutes.

2. a. Mom will be home late. OR
   b. Mom'll be home late.

3. a. Bob will pick us up. OR
   b. Bob'll pick us up.

Part II.
1. The nurse'll give you some medicine.
2. Your headache'll go away quickly.
3. The weather will be nice tomorrow.
4. Sorry, dinner'll be late tonight.
5. The bus will be here in a few minutes.
6. Dad'll help you with your homework later.
7. The students will need more time for review.

Exercise 39, p. 323.
1. Where will you go?
2. When will you go there?
3. Why will you go there?
4. Who will go with you?
5. What will you do there?

Exercise 40, p. 324.
1. Will Samantha study more?
2. Will Samantha go to more parties on weekends?
3. Will Samantha begin smoking?
4. Will Samantha exercise with her grandmother?
5. Will Samantha graduate from a university next year?
6. Will Samantha go on a diet?
7. Will Samantha exercise only two times a week?
8. Will Samantha spend more time with her grandmother?

Exercise 41, p. 324.
1. I want a new car.
2. A new car won't be cheap.
3. You won't get much help from your parents.
4. My parents want me to get married.
5. They want grandchildren.
6. I won't get married for a long time.
7. I want a good education.
8. You won't believe the news!

Exercise 43, p. 326.

A restaurant meal

1. Bert doesn't like meat, eggs, or fish.
2. He's a vegetarian. He doesn't eat meat. He didn't eat it as a child either.
3. His wife, Beth, doesn't eat meat, but she isn't a vegetarian.
4. She doesn't enjoy the taste of meat.
5. They are going to try a new restaurant tomorrow.
6. It opened last month, and online reviews say it is excellent.
7. Bert will probably have a dish with lots of vegetables.
8. Beth won't have vegetables for a main dish. She'll probably ask for some type of fish.
9. Are they going to enjoy themselves?
10. Will they go back to this restaurant?

Exercise 49, p. 330.

Jack and the Beanstalk

NARRATOR: Once upon a time there was a boy named Jack. He lived with his mother in a small village.

MOTHER: We are very poor. We have no money. Our cow has no milk.

JACK: What are we going to do?

MOTHER: You'll go to the market and sell the cow.

NARRATOR: Jack left his home and met an old man on the road.

OLD MAN: I will buy your cow. I will pay you with beans. Here, these are magic beans.

NARRATOR: Jack took the beans home to his mother.

MOTHER: You stupid boy. We have nothing now. We are going to die.

NARRATOR: She threw the beans out the window. The next morning, Jack woke up and saw a huge beanstalk outside his window. It went into the clouds. He decided to climb it. At the top, he saw a castle. Inside the castle, there lived a giant and his wife. He went into the castle.

WIFE: What are you doing? My husband likes to eat boys for breakfast. You need to hide or he will eat you.

JACK: I'm so scared. Please help me.

WIFE: Here, climb inside the oven. After breakfast, my husband will fall asleep.

GIANT: Fee-Fi-Fo-Fum,
I smell the blood of an Englishman.
If he's alive or if he's dead,
I'll use his bones to make my bread.
Hmm. I smell a boy. Wife, are you going to feed me a boy for breakfast?

WIFE: No, I think the smell is the boy from last week. Here's your breakfast.

NARRATOR: The giant ate, counted his gold coins, and soon fell asleep. Jack got out of the oven, took a few gold coins, climbed down the beanstalk, and ran to his mother.

MOTHER: Oh, Jack. You saved us. Now we have money for food. But you are not going to go back to the castle. The giant will eat you.

NARRATOR: But Jack wanted more money. Soon he climbed the beanstalk. Again the giant's wife hid Jack in the oven. The giant had a hen. It laid golden eggs. After the giant fell asleep, Jack stole the hen.

MOTHER: What will we do with a hen? Why didn't you bring more gold coins? Jack, you have no sense.

JACK: Wait, mother. The hen is going to lay a golden egg. Watch.

NARRATOR: The hen laid a golden egg.

MOTHER: Oh, you wonderful boy! We will be rich.

NARRATOR: But Jack wanted more from the giant, so he went up the beanstalk one more time. This time, a golden harp was playing. It made beautiful music. Soon the giant went to sleep, and Jack took the harp. The giant heard a noise and woke up.

GIANT: I will catch you and eat you alive.

NARRATOR: The giant ran after Jack. Jack climbed down the beanstalk. The giant followed. Jack took an axe and chopped down the stalk. The giant fell.

GIANT: Ahhhhhhhhhh!

JACK: The giant is dead.

MOTHER: Now we are safe. The harp will give us beautiful music. My sadness will go away. Our lives will be happy. You saved us!

NARRATOR: And they lived happily ever after.

Chapter 11: Expressing Future Time, Part 2

Exercise 10, p. 339.
1. We may be late for class tomorrow.
2. Your birthday present may come early.
3. Maybe you'll get a package in the mail tomorrow.
4. I may go to bed early tonight.
5. Maybe I'll go shopping tomorrow.
6. Maybe you will get married next year.
7. The weather may be sunny tomorrow.
8. Maybe it will rain tomorrow.

Exercise 13, p. 341.
1. There may be a change in our plans.
2. The weather report says it'll rain tomorrow.
3. We might finish this grammar book soon.
4. Henry may get good news tomorrow.
5. The class'll start on time.

Exercise 26, p. 347.
1. What are you going to do if the weather is nice after class tomorrow?
2. What are you going to do if your teacher cancels class tomorrow?
3. What are you going to do if your teacher begins talking too fast?
4. What are you going to do if you're sick tomorrow?

Exercise 32, p. 351.
1. If I go to bed early tonight,
2. After I get home from school every day,
3. If class finishes early today,
4. Before I eat breakfast every day,
5. After I finish breakfast today,
6. If I get all the answers in this exercise correct,
7. When I finish this grammar book,

Exercise 39, p. 356.
1. A: Are we going to be late for the movie?
   B: No. The movie starts at 7:30. We have plenty of time.

2. A: What are we going to have for dinner?
   B: Leftovers. Is that okay?
   A: Sure, but I'll probably make some rice to go with them.

3. A: Are you going to be at Jon's wedding?
   B: Yes, but I won't get there until after it begins. I work until noon.
   A: Great. I'll see you there.

4. A: What are we going to do? We need to deposit this check, and the cash machine is broken. Our account is almost empty.
   B: No problem. I'll take it with me to work. There's an ATM next door.

Chapter 12: Modals, Part 1: Expressing Ability

Exercise 5, p. 363.
1. a. I can count to 100 in English.
   b. I can't count to 100 in English.

2. a. I can't ride a bike with no hands.
   b. I can ride a bike with no hands.

Exercise 6, p. 364.
1. Some students can't finish the test.
2. The teacher can give you extra help.
3. I can't hear you.
4. You can do it.
5. Don can't work today.
6. The doctor can't see you today.
7. Professor Clark can meet with you tomorrow.
8. I can't find my glasses.
9. The kids can't wait for the party!
10. We can stop now.

Exercise 7, p. 364.
In my last job, I was an office assistant. I have good computer skills. I can do word-processing, and I can type quickly. I like talking to people and can answer the phone with a friendly voice. I also like languages. I can speak French and Chinese. I also studied English. I can read it, but I can't speak it well. I hurt my back a few years ago. I can't carry suitcases. I can work both Saturdays and Sundays.

Exercise 11, p. 366.
1. A: (phone rings) Hello?
   B: Can I speak to Mr. Hudson, please?
   A: I'm sorry. He can't come to the phone right now. Can I take a message? He can return your call in about a half-hour.
   B: Yes. Please tell him Ron Myerson called.

2. A: Can you help me lift this box?
   B: It looks very heavy. I can try to help you, but I think we need a third person.
   A: No, I'm pretty strong. I think we can do it together.

3. A: I can't hear the TV. Can you turn it up?
   B: I can't turn it up. I'm doing my homework.
   A: Can you do your homework in another room?
   B: Oh, all right.

Exercise 26, p. 375.

1. A: Were you able to talk to Adam last night?
   B: I couldn't reach him. I can try again later today.

2. A: Do you know how to make pizza?
   B: Yes, I can make it. What about you?
   A: No, but can you teach me?
   B: Sure.

3. A: Are you able to understand the teacher?
   B: I couldn't understand her in the beginning, but now I can understand most of her lectures.
   A: I still can't understand her very well.

4. A: Professor Castro, when will you be able to correct our tests?
   B: I began last night, but I wasn't able to finish. I'll try again tonight. I hope I will be able to hand them back to you tomorrow.

5. A: (*phone rings*) Hello?
   B: Hi. This is Jan Quinn. I'm wondering if I can get in to see Dr. Novack today or tomorrow.
   A: Well, she can see you tomorrow morning at 11:00. Can you come in then?
   B: Yes, I can. Please tell me where you are. I don't know the way to your office.

Exercise 32, p. 380.
Part III.

1. Dellis can remember long rows of numbers.
2. Dellis is able to memorize a complete deck of cards.
3. In 2011, Dellis was able to win the U.S.A. Memory Championship.
4. Dellis can't remember all this information naturally.
5. Memory champions are able to make pictures in their minds.
6. They say that with a lot of work a person can have a good memory.

Chapter 13: Modals, Part 2: Advice, Necessity, Requests, Suggestions

Exercise 6, p. 387.

1. People should exercise four or five times a week.
2. People should eat a lot of candy.
3. People shouldn't steal money.
4. People should keep some money in a bank.
5. Students should study every day.
6. Students shouldn't study on weekends.
7. English students should speak English in class.
8. English teachers shouldn't translate for their students.

Exercise 12, p. 391.

1. I have to leave early today.
2. You have to come with me.
3. Where does your friend have to go?
4. She has to go to the dentist.
5. My teachers have to correct a lot of homework.
6. Why do they have to give so much work?
7. Our school has to hire a new teacher.
8. My dad has to have surgery.
9. My mom and I have to take him to the hospital tomorrow.
10. He has to stay there for two days.

Exercise 18, p. 395.

1. a. People must eat.
   b. People should eat.

2. a. People should keep their homes clean.
   b. People must keep their homes clean.

3. a. People should stop their cars for a police siren.
   b. People must stop their cars for a police siren.

4. a. People must wear coats in cool weather.
   b. People should wear coats in cool weather.

5. a. People should pay taxes to their government.
   b. People must pay taxes to their government.

6. a. People must drive the speed limit.
   b. People should drive the speed limit.

7. a. People should wear seat belts when they're in a car.
   b. People must wear seat belts when they're in a car.

8. a. People must be polite to one another.
   b. People should be polite to one another.

9. a. People must wear clothes outdoors.
   b. People should wear clothes outdoors.

Exercise 36, p. 406.

1. Tom has to work.
2. Becky knows how to swim.
3. The teacher needed to correct papers.
4. It's a good idea to study for the test tomorrow.
5. We may go to a movie tonight.
6. We didn't have to help.
7. I couldn't go to school yesterday.

Chapter 14: Nouns and Modifiers

Exercise 4, p. 414.
1. Your phone is on the kitchen counter.
2. Your phone is in the kitchen.
3. I'm moving to a new apartment next month.
4. The apartment building has a swimming pool.
5. How do you like your music class?
6. Where are the keys to the car?
7. I'm always losing my car keys.
8. Let's have some chicken soup.
9. The soup is good, but where's the chicken?
10. The grammar in this book is clear.

Exercise 15, p. 424.
1. That was a delicious birthday . . .
2. Here are the car . . .
3. I need to buy some comfortable . . .
4. The teacher gave the class an easy . . .
5. The little boy is playing computer . . .
6. I'd like to read the newspaper . . .

Exercise 31, p. 434.
1. All of the coffee is gone.
2. Some of the coffee is gone.
3. Almost all of the coffee is gone.
4. A lot of the coffee is gone.
5. Most of the coffee is gone.

Exercise 40, p. 441.
1. Most of the people are happy.
2. All of them are smiling.
3. Someone is unhappy.
4. Everyone has a hat.
5. Somebody has sunglasses.
6. Almost all of them look happy.

Chapter 15: Making Comparisons

Exercise 6, p. 448.
1. It's getting cold outside.
2. The weather today is colder than yesterday.
3. I am always colder than you.
4. Our teacher is happier this week than last week.
5. Professor Frank is happy every day.
6. Are you happy today?
7. Is a big car safer than a small car?
8. I want to drive a safe car.
9. I need to get a safer car.
10. The coffee is fresh and tastes delicious.
11. Amy told a very funny story in class yesterday.
12. Amy and Sami both told stories. Sami's story was funnier than Amy's story.

Exercise 14, p. 454.
1. Rudy is older than Alberto.
2. Selena looks happier than Rudy.
3. Alberto is the tallest of all.
4. Selena is younger than Alberto.
5. Rudy looks the most serious.
6. Alberto is shorter than Rudy.
7. Alberto looks happier than Rudy.
8. Rudy is the youngest.
9. Selena is shorter than Alberto.
10. Alberto looks more serious than Selena.

Exercise 17, p. 459.
1. The blue dress is more expensive than the red one.
2. Well, I think the red one looks prettier.
3. Is it too short, or does it look okay?
4. It's the nicest of all the dresses you tried on.
5. I'm not going to buy the brown shoes. They're too small.
6. This hat is too small. I need a bigger size.
7. Here, this is the biggest size they have.
8. I need a belt, but that one is shorter than my old one.
9. Is this belt long enough?
10. It's perfect. And it's the cheapest of all of them.

Exercise 27, p. 468.
1. I work faster than Alec does.
2. Toshi finished his work the fastest of all.
3. Mimi studies harder than Fred.
4. Jean studies the hardest of all.
5. Is a motorcycle more dangerous than a bike?
6. Kalil speaks more loudly than Haruko does.
7. A turtle moves more slowly than a cat does.
8. This suitcase is heavier than that one.
9. My glasses are clearer than my contact lenses.
10. I can see more clearly with my glasses.

Exercise 31, p. 471.
1. B and D are the same.
2. E is different from A.
3. G and B are similar.
4. A is similar to G.
5. F is the same as A.
6. C and G are different.
7. A and C are similar.

Exercise 40, p. 476.
1. Lucy is tall, but her sister is . . .
2. My old apartment was small, but my new apartment is . . .
3. First Street is noisy, but Second Street is . . .
4. This picture is ugly, but that picture is . . .
5. A car is fast, but a bike is . . .
6. A kitten is weak, but a horse is . . .

7. This watch is expensive, but that watch is . . .
8. Oscar is hard-working, but his brother is . . .

Exercise 43, p. 478.

1. I like strong coffee, but my friend . . .
2. Ellen can speak Spanish, but her husband . . .
3. The children didn't want to go to bed early, but their parents . . .
4. The children weren't tired, but their parents . . .
5. Mark doesn't want to go out to eat, but his friends . . .
6. The doctor isn't friendly, but the nurse . . .
7. I was at home yesterday, but my roommate . . .
8. Scott went to the party, but Jerry . . .
9. The grocery store will be open tomorrow, but the bank . . .
10. I won't be home tonight, but my husband . . .

Let's Talk: Answers

Chapter 9, Exercise 12, p. 271.

	wake up	eat for breakfast	spend the day	go to bed	absent
JENNY	(7:00 A.M.)	candy bar	in the library	10 P.M.	Because she had a big project to finish.
JIN	8 A.M.	(rice)	at home	midnight	Because her kids were sick.
JADA	7:00 A.M.	raw fish	(at the beach)	11 P.M.	Because she didn't do her homework.
JANICE	9:00 A.M.	eggs	at the hospital	(10 P.M.)	Because she was in a car accident.
JULIANNA	5:00 A.M.	cold cereal	At her restaurant job	9 P.M.	(Because she needed to earn extra money for school tuition.)

Chapter 12, Exercise 4, p. 363.

1. Yes. [Ostriches and penguins can't fly.]
2. No. [Elephants can't jump.]
3. Yes. [Tigers are very good swimmers.]
4. Yes. [Octopuses change colors when they are excited.]
5. Yes. [The Australian walking fish can climb trees.]
6. No. [Sometimes horses stand up for weeks at a time.]
7. No. [Some turtles can live for 200 or more years.]
8. No. [Some animals see colors, for example, monkeys, birds, and insects.]
9. Yes. [Whales can hold their breath for a long time.]

Index